Love Match

50 Questions to Find your Mate

Steve Brass

© 2013 Steve Brass
Steve Brass — author of Fearless Living

ISBN 10: 1482317532
ISBN 13: 9781482317534

Contact info: www.stevebrass.com or lovematch50@gmail.com

Special dedication to my wonderful wife Donna.

Thanks for sharing the journey of writing this book
and helping me to discover
that you are the most important relationship of my life

Special thanks to my Editors, Catherine Ross
and to Karen Thomas for her cover design.

Much appreciation to those individuals and couples
that shared their views and stories.

Forward

Why another book on relationships you might ask? There are countless books on dating and relationships, but I have never found a resource that offers a checklist of questions to help me recognize the right life partner.

The idea for this book evolved from a recent romance. I had fallen in love with a woman and thought she might be the one. Although I noticed some red flags, I was in a trance in the early stages of the relationship and chose to ignore them.

This trance-like state is very common at the beginning of any new relationship. A trance can be described as "a state of rapture or exaltation in which a person loses their ability to see things rationality and clearly — being in a daze, spell or stupor." We are engulfed in joy and excitement and do not see the other person with clarity or objectivity. We are caught up in a fantasy.

I will refer to this state often in this book, and I suggest you keep it front and center in your mind when "falling" for someone. Not paying attention to early concerns or signs of incompatibility ultimately comes back to bite us.

One morning, after sharing a lovely romantic night, my new love drove me to the airport for an early flight. She kissed me and gave me a big hug. That is the last time I ever spoke to her! Two days later, after numerous phone messages and e-mails asking what was going on, I got an e-mail ending the relationship with no real reason and a refusal to communicate with me. Suddenly, without a word spoken, the relationship was over.

I was dumbstruck and fell into a period of mourning. During the following months of sadness, I regained my balance and reflected on some of the indicators that were obvious during our short three-month romance. I realized that writing down my thoughts and feelings would be a valuable exercise in my healing. I began exploring the important questions I had thought about but was afraid to ask her, or the ones I should have asked myself during the relationship.

After answering these questions honestly, I concluded I had projected my image of what I wanted in a partner and not necessarily what I found in her. I awakened from my trance.

With only fifty percent of marriages lasting and the other half ranging among leaping along happily, limping towards separation, lost in limbo, or stalled in divorce court, I concluded there must be a better way to evaluate who would make a great love match.

Many more people are waiting until their thirties before entertaining marriage. Others have decided marriage is an outdated institution and are content to live with or date someone long-term without a formal and legally binding contract, and some have elected to date or stay single. This book is for those who want a life partner to share this journey.

What clues, qualities and answers do you need to move to the next stage of a serious relationship where you consider a long-term commitment?

I decided to write *Love Match,* and by using fifty questions, I found my mate and was married within a year. We both used this guide to learn about each other, stay conscious and determine our compatibility together. As my wife says jokingly, "It was the worst pick-up line

I had every heard." She was referring to my line about writing a book on how to find a mate. Well, together we used this vehicle as a fun and practical way to get to know each other and it worked.

These fifty questions and your honest answers will help you stay awake so you can recognize that special someone who may become your life mate.

The questions will help you avoid the hurt, confusion, and in some cases, the huge financial losses that can result from making an uneducated decision and marrying someone who might fast track you towards separation and divorce.

After many conversations with friends and strangers of all ages in a variety of relationships, few admitted they thought about using a checklist when in a new relationship, but agreed it was a great idea.

I want to thank those individuals and couples that shared their insights and stories with me. I have gleaned the comments and ideas they provided and changed their names for privacy reasons, but all the quotes and experiences shared are true to the best of my recollection.

Some of the on-line dating sites have psychological profiles and assessments. Having joined a few briefly, I found very few candidates even close to what I was seeking. I concluded they were a nice marketing twist, but hardly a tool I would use for my pursuit of a life mate.

The notion of finding a soul mate is a long shot, and more common in fiction and on screen. Yes, we hear of people meeting and within days or weeks creating a lifelong marriage. My new in-laws are an example of this. After just three weeks of meeting, they married and have enjoyed a strong union for over forty years. I believe they are the rare exception.

A checklist for the most important relationship of your life is both a sensible and required tool.

The book is divided into these five pillars or sections: Chemistry• Cash • Communication • Caring • Commitment

Compatibility is the foundation of this book and the questions rest on five pillars:

1. Chemistry
2. Cash
3. Communication
4. Caring
5. Commitment

Having just one of these five pillars standing strong is not enough to support a long-term relationship. An example comes from, Margie, one of the first women that I interviewed.

"Oh, the sex is incredible, she said. "But he criticizes me a lot and he's always late for appointments."

"What's the most important thing to you in your relationship?" I asked.

She looked at me, truly stumped. She had not stopped to think about her priorities in her life.

What kind of relationship do you truly want? Sexual chemistry is great, but what about your financial compatibility, communication styles, your degree of commitment and your level of caring for each other?

Avoiding these questions can lead to disappointment, a loss of time and a depleted bank account.

When I was single, I met some lovely women and felt an instant physical attraction. It only took a short conversation about their lifestyles to find out they were not even close to a match for me. Conversations like this have saved me from investing time, energy, and heartache in a relationship doomed before it started.

Before you get side-tracked by a surge in hormones, a nice ass or a great smile, stop. Ask yourself some simple questions. The voice in your head should ask, "What do I like about this person?" Then, "Am I attracted by physical appearance or is there something intriguing about this person's personality that makes me want to invest my time and energy in getting to know them?" Of course if you are looking for a good time and not a long time, this book is probably not your best guide.

From there, the questions in this book flow. Are your lifestyles compatible? Do you think about money in the same way? Are you both financially self-supporting or is one or both of you a financial wreck? Can you communicate with each other? Do you speak your mind and expect the same from the other person? Or does one of you have a tough time saying what it is on you mind? Is one of you a people pleaser? Are you both honest with your feelings and confident to confront uncomfortable issues if needed? Do you hide behind a cheery façade or do you let those you have true feelings for into your heart?

How would you rate your level of commitment to this relationship? Are you interested in someone to date occasionally, a movie pal, a casual friend for an occasional sexual encounter, or a truly intimate monogamous life partner?

It may take a while to discover how compatible you are, but being aware of these questions will help determine if this person might be your love match. The more favorable answers you receive from these fifty questions the better chance you have of sustaining a passionate, kind, and committed union.

I have provided space at the end of each question to write your impressions and a scale to rate your compatibility with this person.

Yes, some of the answers you receive to your questions may not be what you want to hear because it rocks your fantasy. Again, take your time and give this the attention and consideration it truly deserves. Making a rash decision can leave you emotionally and financially in ruins.

It is not always easy to be honest with our motives and needs when dating. We may be scared to be alone, but loneliness is a poor excuse to give your heart, body and wallet to someone. We may simply believe now is the time to be married, but finding a suitable life partner requires time, effort, negotiation and compromise.

Gerry was the only person I interviewed whose honesty led him to the decision to give up on finding a relationship. He admitted to me that he was not very astute or successful in recognizing a good love match. Gerry has been divorced three times. Those divorces had steep financial and emotional consequences. Because he is financially secure, he made a decision to pay for social company. Instead of dating, he arranges escorts.

You've picked up this book because you are not like Gerry. You have not given up. You know the euphoric first stage of any relationship usually fades within months or at best a couple of years. Then you wake up and see someone who also has shortcomings, issues and challenges you may not have consciously seen or chosen to admit to yourself earlier.

The fairy tale feeling is sometimes too overwhelming that we became lost in our own story of what we dreamed of instead of what we are living.

Anyone who does not want to talk about compatibility by addressing sex, money, religion, children, parenting, and communication styles is either afraid, hiding something, or immature.

If you find there are too many differences, hurdles or deal breakers between you, then the price of this project is a small one compared to the possible costs you may expend down the road.

However, if after taking this survey your answers confirm your strong heartfelt feelings for this new person, coupled with compatibility on many levels, you may have hit the jackpot and found your mate.

There is space at the end of each question for both you and your partner to record your thoughts and feelings. There is also a rating scale at the end of each question for you to circle. 1, 3 or 5. 1 indicating LITTLE OR NO compatibility to a score of 3, being SOMEWHAT compatible, to a 5 which means VERY compatible. I have included an opportunity for you to write your own fiftieth question at the end of the book. What question would you ask a new person or ask yourself about them?

I hope this adventure proves to be full of fun, discovery and passion as you move closer to finding your Love Match. I welcome your comments and stories-lovematch50@gmail.com

Here are a few words from my Love Match.

My husband and I met the old-fashioned way. We were introduced by mutual friends. Although I had come close to getting married a couple of times, at 48, I had never been married.

Like so many other single adults, I had been bumping through dates guided by a general picture of what I wanted in a relationship.

*In the couple of years before I met Steve, I had been looking for compatibility help with one of the on-line dating services. Although I met some genuinely nice men, I did not meet anyone who was right for me. My experience was that any compatibility, match, or screening offered turned out to be superficial. If I did meet someone **who was smart** and interesting, I found out he had a two-year old child. Or debt collectors.*

Or contempt for my religion. Or a spouse. That is, we were not compatible for any long-term relationship.

I was learning by trial and error, a lot of error, that having a general picture of what I wanted didn't work. It was not enough. I needed to be more focused on the qualities, character traits and deal-breakers that were important to me.

In one of our early phone conversations, Steve enchanted me with what I still call the worst pick-up line of all time.

"It's all about the questions," he said about compatibility. "I've been studying this for over a year. Now I'm writing a book called 'Love Match-50 Questions to find your mate."

It was more that having similar experiences in dating people who were not right. Steve did something about it. He focused on questions as a tool for exploring compatibility – questions to ask yourself and to ask a potential mate.

As our relationship started, all the questions were fair game. We worked through all of them, plus a few bonus questions. My favorite question? That was when Steve asked me to marry him

- Donna Brass

We welcome your stories at www.stevebrass.com

Contents

The five pillars of compatibility:

5. COMMITMENT - Questions 42-49   191

Share your questions and experiences with lovematch50@gmail.com

COMPATIBILITY SCALE

Chemistry Cash Communication Caring Commitment

Using this scoring system will help you evaluate the pillars of compatibility as you navigate the many dimensions of getting to know someone new. The more 3's and 5's you recognize the better probability you have of growing this romance into a serious committed relationship which may blossom into discovering your life mate.

Pillar One: Chemistry

Question 1

Chemistry

What type of relationship are you seeking?

Knowing what you want in a relationship dramatically increases your chances of getting there. It may seem like an obvious question, but many of the people I spoke with seemed to stumble through relationships without knowing what they wanted.

Are you looking for a short-term romance, a friend with benefits, or a long-term committed union? Would you prefer not to date right now and instead enjoy your time alone or in the company of friends and family?

Knowing what you want when someone appears in your life will help to determine if this person is worth the investment of time and energy. If you are on the same page, you can proceed and explore the dance of a new relationship. However, if you are in very different places, be cautious, because if the chemistry overwhelms or clouds your judgment, and you decide to venture forth with this person, you may have a rude awakening when you realize you were not listening when they told you what they were seeking.

Some people think they can change someone to fit their agenda. Bad idea. Others, blinded by their fantasy, neglect to hear, see or accept that the other person is not heading in the same direction. You can probably name someone, maybe even yourself, who has done this.

Frank, in his early fifties, told me that he finally figured it out. He is financially secure, with no kids, splitting his residence between summer and winter climates. He explained that he recently met a very attractive woman at a community event, and immediately felt a strong physical attraction. As he got to know her, he steered the conversation toward a few areas that were his priorities. Using a few targeted questions, he quickly realized that their lives were on very different pages. She was unemployed, just divorced, and lived with her two teenage daughters. Yes, he could have followed the physical attraction, but he knew the outcome would be short-lived. He did not want to get emotionally involved with someone who could not join him in his life and lifestyle. Frank says he's been down that route and has the t-shirt to prove it. He admits he is grateful that he now makes more conscientious choices.

Chris is even more straightforward with the women he meets. He knows exactly what he wants. Here's his pitch: "I like you and if you want to hang out, that's great. I am free on weekends for a good time. I will not call you during the week; I will not text; I don't want to know the details of your day, and I really am not interested in knowing if you are dating other people. You know how to contact me if you want to get together. No pressure. No plans."

I commend Chris on his straightforward, albeit cold, approach. There are no games, hidden agendas or deceptions with Chris. Any woman who is interested can freely decide if this is the kind of man or relationship she wants. Any woman who thinks, "Oh I can change all that," is dreaming and is setting herself up for huge disappointment.

Some of the women I spoke with were equally straightforward. Susan, a single, professional, financial planner in her early 30s, tells the men she meets, "I have no interest in getting married or having kids. Anyone who wants marriage and a family knows this is not the bus stop for them." Susan added that anyone who tries to convince her otherwise is a fool and she has met her share.

Some may say they aren't sure about what kind of relationship they are looking for and will just wait and see how things unfold. While, that may work for some, it gets more difficult as you get older, more set in your own life. Spending some time honestly thinking about your own needs and wants makes it easier to see if there is a future with this person. Yes, sometimes we unexpectedly discover some qualities that change our position and what we want, and that is a bonus, but if we go in with our eyes and ears wide open and have a checklist, we will be pleasantly surprised and encouraged when our pillars begin to line up.

Are you looking for a monogamous relationship? What does monogamy mean to you? Does it mean you remain sexually committed and exclusive to one partner? Does it determine how you spend time with friends of the opposite sex? Does it limit travel plans, visiting or social activities with members of the opposite sex whom you may have known for some time? A lady I was dating asked me not to see my female friends for a while, so we could focus on our relationship. I reluctantly agreed, because I was in that trance-like early phase of romantic attraction, and I wanted to explore this new relationship. The decision cost me some very dear and long-time friends. Was my new lady's request due to her own insecurity, a control tactic, or a genuine desire to focus on us first? She agreed to stop seeing her male friends socially without me – or so she said. I understand her request to spend more time with me, but asking me not to see old friends made me uncomfortable. However, I chose to ignore my feelings and did not stand my ground. You can guess how that ended.

What is your sexual preference? If you are straight, gay or bisexual, and do not communicate this clearly to someone new, that can only lead to confusion, pain and trouble.

We have heard of the situation where after several years of marriage (sometimes with children) a spouse confesses that he/she is gay/lesbian and wants out of the relationship. Some individuals secretly suppress their homosexuality and marry for appearance or cultural pressure. Some couples that are fully aware of their partner's different sexual orientation still proceed with a traditional male/female marriage. Because marriage has enough hurdles to surmount, it is important to be clear that this is a conscious choice.

This was clear when Greg shared with me that he had met Roxanne in a club and there was an instant sexual charge between them. They jumped into bed that night and began a torrid relationship. They were both quick to state to each other that they did not want a long term or exclusive relationship. After two months, Roxanne admitted she was in love with Greg and wanted to spend more time with him. Greg told me, "I have to figure out a way to end this."

They were on different pages with opposing wants. Sometimes, we can change our hearts and minds about what we want with someone, but this was not the case with Greg.

While I was having dinner with a friend who was going through an ugly divorce, she told me that she had found herself attracted to women. We talked about her vulnerability going through the divorce. She found women more emotionally accessible and supportive. She was struggling with the feelings of being nourished by her girlfriends, and wondering if she was physically attracted to them too.

A romantic relationship has a natural flow and if the pillars do not line up, move on.

This was clear when I spoke with Ian, a young urban planner. He told me he had met a nice, single woman he was attracted to and began hanging out with her hoping it would evolve into something romantic. After months of spending time together, he told me he was frustrated because she was sending mixed messages about what she wanted in a relationship. I cut to the chase and asked him, "Why hasn't the relationship progressed beyond flirty-friendship after all this time?" As we continued to talk, it became clear that the signals were not mixed. It was clear. She was not interested in a romantic relationship and he was wasting his time and energy focusing on this woman instead of moving on.

Ian was caught in that trance of what he wanted to see. He could not look beyond this to realize the woman did not share his dream. Sometimes it is easier to play inside your fantasy than accept the truth about the situation. Ian snapped out of his trance. If you find yourself lamenting with your friends about all the challenges and delays in reaching that special place you long to create with a new person you have chemistry with, then it is time to take a hard look at what you are willing to accept or not.

Daniela describes relationships like a meal. She asks, "Is this person an appetizer, the entree or just dessert?" Once you know what course you want it is easier to decide where to dine.

What type of relationship are you seeking?

_____

_____

_____

What type of relationship is your partner seeking?

Circle your compatibility score   1   3   5

Question 2

Chemistry

Do you have chemistry with this person?

Most couples are initially drawn together by a physical attraction – a sexual spark that begins the dance of talking, laughing, dating and intimacy. Science shows that a chemical reaction heightens our interest in someone and then we enter into a trance-like attraction that propels us forward into romance.

One of the critical pillars of compatibility, which this book rests on, is a strong foundation of romantic chemistry. The sexual pull may initially be the strongest, but in time it is important to evaluate other aspects of connection.

How easy is your conversation? Are you the one always initiating the dialogue, or is there a comfortable flow of topics between you? Do you have similar interests that strengthen your bond?

Do your plans run smoothly or is one person hard to contact, indecisive and always late?

Charles met a woman at a party. They had an immediate physical attraction and fun chatting with a little flirting thrown in for good measure. He asked her out on a date. From the first invitation, she gave reasons why each time what he suggested would not work. Eventually, he realized that despite her projected willingness, she was not available for the kind of relationship he was seeking. How many of us would have pursued this person anyway only to find out in one or two dates that they were not truly available?

Fran tells me, she met a nice guy, went out on a couple of dates, had great conversation, laughter, and then suddenly he stopped calling. She thought there was a physical connection based on his smiles, touches and a little kissing. Then it just stopped. She made an effort to see him again but received one excuse after another about his other plans that did not include her. When she realized that she was making all the effort to carry the relationship forward and stopped those efforts, she never heard from him again. Although she was disappointed, she told me that she was thankful that she avoided a pending romantic drama. It takes two to make chemistry flow and if one party cannot decide, keeps backing up or sends mixed messages, it is better to be alone until the right fit comes along.

People like Fran and Charles were a warning not to be fooled by a chemical reaction that sends you into that trance-like state. At first glance, someone appears to be sexy, attractive or interesting. If you are looking for a date, that may be enough. But if you are looking for a lasting relationship, these fifty questions can help you to move beyond the superficial and help you recognize significant mate material for you.

Are your relationship goals compatible? Beyond the initial spark, is there a continued desire to get to know each other, or are there obstacles preventing you from getting to know each other?

Max's story about meeting a woman at a networking event is an example of stumbling-along in an attempt to get know someone. He says, "I was attracted by her looks. We chatted, exchanged phone numbers and made a date to get together." They went for a hike in a local park. Max told me he was encouraged by the easy conversation with playful banter. When they returned to the parking lot, he moved to give her a hug. Although he was surprised when she stepped away to avoid his hug, he assumed she needed more than one date before she was comfortable hugging him. He called her a couple of days later and asked her to a concert. She agreed. He told me the date was awkward from the beginning and got worse. When he tried to engage in conversations about her work and family, she resisted. She flatly refused to tell him her last name. Max admitted to me that because he was still caught in his desire to get to know this woman, he persisted.

Max e-mailed her a few times with no reply. Still not willing to give up, he called to ask if she received his e-mails. She claimed she never received them. He asked her what she was doing the following week-end. When she told him that her children were visiting, but she "could fit him in between two and four p.m. on Sunday." He snapped out of his trance. They never spoke again.

Gene's story is another example of this stumbling along in an attempt to get know someone.

Gene went to a sports clinic for a check-up on an ankle injury where he met Bella in the reception area. While waiting, they began a casual conversation about sports injuries and their mutual like of hiking. He found her easy to talk to and he asked for her phone number. She gave him her card and the next day he phoned to invite her to lunch. She agreed on a time to meet him on the following Saturday, but then called to say she had remembered previous plans for the day and had to put him off until later. Gene understood and asked her to call him as the day unfolded to get together later. She never called. Like Max, he was not ready to give up. He e-mailed her a couple of days later asking her out again. She agreed, then at the last minute cancelled. He told me that he didn't want to be treated this way and told her it was best if they stopped their email exchanges. Bella apologized pro-fusely and insisted she did want to go out with him. Max was reluctant, but she offered to pick him up for a sunset picnic. Appreciating the effort, Gene agreed.

Gene was impressed when Bella arrived on time. They went to a beautiful canyon in the hills. She had packed a lovely dinner with wine and chocolate dessert. They sat under the stars talking comfortably for hours. Gene told me that he was glad that he took another chance to get to know her. That is until she dropped the bomb on Gene – Bella had a boyfriend. He asked her why she had made such a romantic picnic if she had a boyfriend. She replied, "I'm not sure what I want with him so I thought I would spend some time with you." This is a perfect example of an initial physical attraction that some would call chemistry, that quickly turned into an incompatible misfire. Gene realized his standard of care was very different from Bella's. They finished their evening and he made no effort to contact her again.

True chemistry includes much more than physical attraction. Do not be lured into the strongest and usually the temporary pull of sexual attraction; instead, consider the five pillars of compatibility and create a strong, lasting relationship.

Do you have chemistry with this person?

_____

_____

_____

Circle your compatibility score   1   3   5

Question 3

Chemistry

Do you like your body?

We live in a society obsessed with the perfect body, the right diet, the latest fashion, and the ideal exercise regime. Such high expectations can make accepting yourself a real challenge. How you feel about your body and what you are willing to do to achieve a specific look can present issues for both yourself and a potential partner. Acknowledging how you feel about your own body can help you initiate discussion with your partner in identifying potential intimacy issues.

I have known women who readily admit that they are afraid to undress in front of their partner or even get into bed before turning off the lights. Like me, you have known women who make endless comments critical of their nose, lips, hips, breast or any other aspect of their appearance. The same is true of men. I have male friends who tell me that they spend too much time obsessing with their appearance before leaving the house. As I spoke with men and women about body consciousness, they helped me realize that opening this dialogue can reveal significant image issues that can impact your chemistry.

Sasha shared with me that she often engaged in sex with men on the first date. When I asked her about this behavior, she said, " That's the only way guys will like me."

Colleen admitted to me that she did not like her body and was hesitant to kiss or touch anyone she was dating because it may lead to deeper intimacy, which made her uncomfortable.

These two women represent opposite ends of the body image spectrum. Sasha was free and easy with sex while Colleen was reserved when it comes to affection and intimacy.

Ted's story was a little different. When he began dating Lila, their initial attraction and common interests progressed into an intimate relationship. After a few weeks of intimacy, Ted realized that Lila was only affectionate when she drank a bottle or more of wine. Despite Ted's assurances that he found her attractive she was unable to unwind without this crutch. This was a warning sign, Ted told me. Shortly after recognizing this behavior, he broke off the relationship.

From my conversations, it became apparent that this is a question to ask yourself before approaching the topic with your partner. Acknowledging how you feel about your body then talking with your partner can help you recognize any potential land mines with your chemistry and future intimacy

Pam realized this about her relationship with Rick. Pam told me he was reluctant to eat out or even share a meal together. When they did share a meal, she commented that he ate like a bird. He claimed he was not hungry, but later she learned that Rick's ex-wife had been critical of his weight for their entire marriage and he continued to struggle with his self-image. Pam really enjoyed eating out and socializing with friends. This was not the relationship she wanted with Rick and chose not to see him anymore.

These stories emphasized the importance of an inward focused question in examining chemistry with a partner. Sometimes these questions are strictly for us and sometimes they can lead to a jumping off point of discussion with our partner.

The other thing these stories emphasized was the importance of not judging the other person. Rather, judge whether that person is a good love match for you.

Do you like your body?

_____

_____

_____

Does your partner like their body?

_____

_____

_____

Circle your compatibility score   1   3   5

Question 4

Chemistry

How comfortable are you sharing a sexual fantasy?

Although a person's fantasy can be anything from climbing Mt Everest, retiring to Bali or writing a book, this section focuses on sexual fantasy. The answers to this question could add spice to a new relationship, clarify your partner's desires or reveal something that makes you uncomfortable.

Janice told me about her relationship with Jerome. She described their relationship as meeting on weekends for some fun and casual sex. One night he shared his fantasy — a threesome with her and another man. This was definitely not the experience she wanted or was willing to accommodate. When she told me this story, she admitted she was open to a threesome – but with another woman. Their relationship ended that day when Jerome admitted he preferred men.

We all have sexual fantasies that can increase our enjoyment of each other – a three-some is just Janice's example. Depending on how much trust and honesty has occurred in a new relationship, you may or may not want to share them. I think if you have strong fantasies that you want to share with a partner, you should confess them earlier rather than later. You risk driving your lover away if your fantasy turns out to be too strange or uncomfortable for them. By discussing your sexual wants, you both reveal how comfortable you are with your body and your willingness to express your sexuality with your new love.

How easy is it to flirt with your new love? Are they receptive? Playfulness can be a big turn on, but if you are the one making all the effort, that could be a warning sign. Your willingness to flirt may be a sign of your level of play and affection you can share with your partner. If you are a touchy feely person who likes to give hugs and kisses but your partner does not initiate affection in this way, it may frustrate you. A conversation about this eventually may help you develop a dialogue about fantasy.

Mike's story was an example of this type of conversation. He told me that he was in a long-term relationship with Penny, but questioned their chemistry. Penny never initiated sex, but was open when Mike did. Mike's fantasy was for Penny to seduce him. He realized he wanted this relationship to continue and chose to communicate his fantasy. This led to a new level of sharing in their relationship and Penny began making more effort in the bedroom.

Exploring this question helps give you an idea of your future physical chemistry.

How comfortable are you sharing a sexual fantasy?

_____

_____

_____

How comfortable is your partner sharing a sexual fantasy?

_____

_____

_____

Circle your compatibility score   1   3   5

Question 5

Chemistry

What level of intimacy do you desire?

What level of intimacy do you want for your new relationship? This is not an easy question to answer, but knowing what you want helps to achieve the depth of sharing and commitment you desire with this new person.

Actress Jane Fonda, at the age of 72, said it took her three marriages and numerous relationships to realize what true intimacy is. She caught my attention while she was doing a television interview. She described intimacy as feeling open, vulnerable yet comfortable enough with herself that she could reveal all parts of her being to her lover without fear of being judged or abandoned.

Her comments resonated with me because intimacy is not just how sexually open you are, although that is a critical aspect. Can you trust yourself and your partner to truly reveal yourselves to each other? This can be threatening as some fear reprisal, embarrassment or abandonment.

For some partners, it is enough to talk about day-to-day routine. They have no desire to delve into anything more open or vulnerable. For others, exploring a closer, soulful connection is the goal of a committed relationship.

In another interview, Jeff Bridges, the Oscar-winning actor, was asked how he had sustained his marriage for over thirty years in a world where most couples head for the door at the first road bump. He explained that he and his wife had learned early that each time they hit a wall and wanted to leave, it was an opportunity to take another step towards intimacy and learning.

Listening to these two celebrities discuss intimacy illustrated what I found to be a common theme in my conversations throughout this project. Having the freedom to share your greatest fears, regrets, dreams and goals with the confidence your lover is there for you, creates a nourishing partnership like no other. Knowing what level of intimacy you desire is important in finding the right match. Although we do not always know to what depth we are willing to expose ourselves, having the trust to explore the most sensitive regions of our being with a lover can be a great adventure. It takes time and experience for both partners to recognize and feel comfortable with this intimate dance.

The "Dance of Intimacy" says author and therapist, Harriet Lerner, is a common process in new relationships. When we have demons or fears and want to test our new partner, Dr. Lerner says, "we will cautiously drop a small bomb on their lap to see their reaction". If they stay, the next piece of information we share might be even more explosive. Again, this tests their willingness to accept and love us or run for the hills.

Thomas' story was a painful one that reflects this Dance of Intimacy. After a few dates with Diane, she told him that her foster parent had abused her. This saddened Thomas, but he offered support and comfort. A few weeks later after a few glasses of wine, Diana told Thomas that her ex-husband had raped her then emptied their bank account before he left. Again, Thomas was shocked, angry at the actions of her ex, and tried to comfort her. Eventually, he realized she was testing his interest and desire to be with her, because on some level, she may have felt unworthy of his love and care. She was used to having men use and abuse her. Thomas tried to show her he was not that kind of man, but this did not convince her and the more time they spent together the more bombshells she hurled onto his lap. Thomas confessed to me, "Diana's emotional needs were greater than I could handle." She needed the expertise of a therapist. Thomas realized that his efforts were inadequate and he chose to step away from the relationship.

What level of intimacy do you desire?

_____

_____

_____

What level of intimacy does your partner desire?

_____

_____

_____

Circle your compatibility score   1   3   5

Question 6

Chemistry

What are your plans for children?

Do you have children? Do you want children? Or have you decided not to become a parent?

Knowing what you want regarding children makes it easier to decide if this new person is a good fit for your future plans.

Many have a strong desire to be a parent while others do not. Again, this is not about judging the choices others make. Rather, this is about judging the right match for your love. The key is honestly communicating your preference to a potential mate.

Hannah, a thirty-nine-year-old school teacher was still unsure if she wanted a child or not. The man she was dating was clear that he did not want to be a parent. This open dialogue helped them make the decision about a future together.

After a nine-month separation, Steven started dating Susan, a single woman. She was attracted to him, but uncomfortable with his marital status. When Susan voiced her concerns, Steven assured her that his wife was living in another country and they were not getting back together. Steven and Susan agreed they both wanted a family. Yet regardless of his assurances, Susan decided she wanted someone who was free and clear to focus on their relationship.

If you do not have children, are you okay with dating someone who does? If so, you may discover you enjoy this new role and in time become a great step-parent.

Harry was ready, willing and able to be a step-parent when he fell in love with Gwen, who had two children living with her. Harry was very fond of her kids, he told me, but realized early that he and Gwen had different ideas about discipline and respect. This became an ongoing issue of disagreement between them, which left Harry feeling out of place since they were not his children. In Harry's opinion, Gwen failed to teach her children about cleaning up after themselves, helping with household chores and speaking appropriately to adults. He witnessed their disrespect for their mother and their home. When he tried to offer ideas to help resolve some of the tension in the home he was met with, "You're not our father so we don't have to listen to you." Harry replied, "That's true, but I am an adult and I would like some respect." Gwen who had become accustomed to this relationship with her kids sided with them. Eventually Harry decided it was too much and left.

If you have children, are they still living with you? Does your partner have children and what is their status (sole or shared custody, living nearby or in another city)? Will your two families blend easily? Do you and your children get along with your partner's children? Are you considering co-habitation? Will one of you need to sell your home, or are you comfortable moving into another residence, especially if it is the home of your partner's ex-spouse? Thoughtful consideration of these questions will help to defuse potential landmines.

Bruce learned about negotiation and compromise when he started dating Charmaine. He was divorced with two kids living with him. Charmaine also had two children living with her. Both their ex-spouses were sore spots when planning weekends and family outings. Over time, Bruce and Charmaine negotiated and scheduled time alone together when their children were visiting their ex-spouses. Bruce admitted he was not crazy about Charmaine's kids. His children were a little older and did not find much in common with her kids. They realized that it would be some time before they could entertain sharing a home together and were happy seeing each other as much as they could.

Lawrence is another story of successful negotiation. He is Jewish. He fell in love with Jean, a Catholic woman. She wanted to get married and have children. So did he. However, it was a priority for him that she convert and raise their children in the Jewish faith. She agreed, and they have been married for many years with two great kids

In my conversations with couples, the topic of older parents came up numerous times.

People who are caretakers for their parents or other relatives, who may live with them, have additional demands on their time and energy which can impact a relationship. Keep these factors in mind in the early stages of a new relationship.

What are your plans for children?

_____

_____

_____

What are your partner's plans for children?

_____

_____

_____

Circle your compatibility score   1   3   5

Question 7

Chemistry

Do you have fun with your partner?

How often do you laugh together? How easy is it for you to be silly and let the worries of the day fall away and just relax and play together? Can you make a trip to the hardware store, the ice cream shop or a movie an adventure?

Life is tough and the challenges can hit hard sometimes. Having a buddy to laugh with who can bring you back to a balanced place with a silly smile, a joke or a wild gesture, is a plus.

Conversely, take note of someone who is always partying, being silly and goofing around. They may not be willing or capable of having a serious conversation, managing a crisis, or being there for you when the chips are down. There are some individuals who are looking for a parent to handle the grown up responsibilities and would rather remain in their youthful mind-set while you mind the adult store.

Jessie met Todd, a windsurfing coach. He was fun, attractive and fit. After a month, he announced that he had found a job overseas coaching at an international surfing event. When we talked, Jessie told me that she didn't even know he was considering a move.

She could not afford to join him and remained working in a clothing store in their town. Although they were apart, she remained excited about this romance. When I asked her what he would be doing after the competition was over. She replied, "I don't know. We didn't talk about it much."

"Did you talk about seeing each other and continuing your relationship?" I asked.

"Not really," she answered.

From our conversation, it was clear that Jessie believes she is in love and expects a relationship when he returns. I wondered if she had projected her desire into a fantasy of what their future would be without consulting him.

Having someone to laugh and enjoy life with is paramount for some. Having a partner who can also share paying the bills, care for you in sickness, or provide counsel if your career takes a turn is also an important priority in choosing a mate. Being involved with someone who is often serious, reserved and does not express themselves openly with words or affection may eventually wear thin. Finding the balance between someone who can be playful and still responsible is an important consideration in your choice of a love match.

The question "Do you have fun with this person?" goes beyond the bedroom. Yes, lovemaking should be pleasurable, mutual and fun, but in the day-to-day experience of your relationship, do you have fun together?

I have dated women who enjoyed my humor and found my accents, characters and silliness entertaining, but rarely joined me in my antics. I found this got old fast. I wanted someone with whom to share my lighter side. One of the big ingredients that helped me find love with my wife is her ability to flow with the playfulness and just let her professional face go when we are together. She accepted my silly side and I was very attracted to hers. We have great chemistry in the fun department and this adds to our love for each other. We found our balance.

Do you have fun with your partner?

_____

_____

_____

Does your partner have fun with you?

_____

_____

_____

Circle your compatibility score   1   3   5

Question 8

Chemistry

How important are your religious/ spiritual beliefs in your relationship?

Do you have a strong faith in a God or a higher power? Do you belong to a church, temple or place of worship that is an important part of your life?

Finding someone who is comfortable with a faith system and can accept and partake in yours can add great chemistry to the relationship. If one of you has no affiliation with a religion or does not believe in a higher power and this is an intimate part of your being, this may present some challenges.

If you and your new love do not have strong religious ties or are atheists, this question may not be an issue at all.

If one person believes their religion is the only way to heaven and is critical of other faith systems, they may be waving a huge red flag. Some people will tell you flat out that if you are not a member of their church they cannot date you. Others will only entertain meeting or dating someone who is from the same race, culture or academic background.

Gayle told me she was terrified of telling her family of born-again Christians, that she had fallen in love with a Muslim man. She loved spending time with him and found his religion fascinating and in many ways similar to her own. The challenge for Gayle was broaching the subject of loving someone outside her faith with her family. Her boyfriend was quite accepting of her beliefs, but realized the difficulty of her position with her family.. He did not pressure her to make a decision, and in time, she realized the best choice for her was to pursue the relationship, risking the consequences of her family's reactions.

My friend Moshe served in the Israeli army during the 1967 war with Egypt and had fought against Arabs on the front lines. We were watching a news report on another violent episode between the Palestinians and the Israelis. He turned to me and said, "Do you know how they can solve this endless conflict?" I was intrigued and asked how? "They should all marry each other so they could get on to more important things than fighting," he replied.

From my conversations, it became clear to me that if someone is very close to their family, have deep cultural or religious ties, you are not just gaining a lover but inheriting their extended circle. In some cases, this means specific dietary requirements, social commitments, family obligations and financial investment.

Laine worked as an administrator in her children's Christian school. She was in a relationship with a man who initially accepted her commitment to the school's Christian community. Then she began to notice a change to the point where he demanded Laine assume the role of a woman as described in a specific interpretation of the Old Testament. Although this change shocked Laine, she told me that she was clear in her religious beliefs and the role of those beliefs in her relationship. That made it easy for her to walk away from what, until then, had been a promising relationship.

Sally's story is opposite from Laine's. For Sally, it is important for her to go to church on Christmas and Easter. Richard, her new love, does not want to be confined to one religious group. Early on, he told Sally that his favorite church is being outside in nature. He accompanies her to church twice a year and they each respect their different approaches to God. Sally told me that she is confident that she and Richard have discussed this difference and found a mutually respectful approach to this aspect of their relationship.

One more story of mutual respect comes from Maxine. Maxine described herself as a non-religious person with no desire or need to follow a specific belief system. She met and fell in love with Marty, who was a devout Buddhist. She gave him the freedom to go to his temple and practice his faith in a way that was important to him. He didn't try to imprint his beliefs on her. They developed a mutually respectful routine that provides time for Marty to meditate early every morning while Maxine is still asleep. Most mornings, Maxine tells me, Marty has the newspaper and coffee ready for her when she awakes.

Finding someone with a similar religious or spiritual belief or is comfortable with how you practice (or don't) yours can add great chemistry to the relationship.

How important are your religious/spiritual beliefs in your relationship?

_____

_____

_____

How important are your partner's religious/spiritual beliefs in your relationship?

_____

_____

_____

Circle your compatibility score   1   3   5

Question 9

Chemistry

Are you happy around this person?

When you think of your new love, do you feel happy and excited about seeing, embracing and sharing time with them? Does a smile come to your face? Does their presence add to your happiness and feeling of self -worth or are you fooling yourself to avoid being alone on a Saturday night?

This is not an easy question for some to answer. If you are struggling with this one, I suggest you step back and consider whether you can envision a better future knowing this person is by your side.

Are you generally happy on your own? Depending on another to make you happy has risks. If you place your happiness in their hands, what happens if they leave, change or die? Many people I interviewed stressed that happiness begins with them.

Francis voiced her opinion on happiness with me by saying, "Love multiplies, and being with someone should open your heart and bring a feeling of joy when you think of them in your life." I believe this is true for how they add to your sense of happiness too. Do you feel better around them?

If you are struggling with concerns about this person, that is quite okay, provided they are not deal breakers. Can you honestly say they add to your happiness and you truly enjoy their company? Every couple will have issues that must be explored and resolved. It will not always be a ride on party avenue, although in the early stages of the trance/dance, we sometimes trick ourselves into believing this euphoric state will never change.

Every person I spoke with who was happy with their relationship agreed that they were happy around their partner.

Everyone has experienced walking into a room full of people and immediately feeling a sense of ease and warmth or the opposite – tension and discomfort. Part of the process of falling in love includes a new circle of friends and an extended family. Does this new group of people add to the happiness you feel around your partner or present a challenge?

Are you happy around this person?

_____

_____

_____

Is this person happy around you?

_____

_____

_____

Circle your compatibility score   1   3   5

Question 10

Chemistry

Do you prefer healthy food or the Drive Through?

Are your lifestyles on the same page?

Sharing meals with your partner consumes a fair portion of your time together. Are your diets compatible? If one person is a vegan and very conscious and disciplined about what they ingest, and the other eats on the run and has little interest in nutrition or healthy food options, challenges may arise.

How we nourish our bodies indicates our standard of care for ourselves. Our health is our responsibility and how we treat our bodies may extend into how we treat others and their needs.

Are your needs for physical activity compatible? If one is a couch potato and the other has a daily exercise regime, your time together may be limited. Are your work and sleep schedules compatible? If one partner does shift work or one suffers from sleep apnea and needs to wear a special mask connected to a noisy machine, sharing one bed could pose problems.

In the early romantic stage of a new relationship, we do not see or choose to overlook some of the lifestyle issues facing the relationship. If you are committed to a healthy diet and regular exercise and sleep, and choose not to smoke, drink or take drugs and your partner does not share your choices, be aware of this earlier rather than later. Someone who influences or tries to change your lifestyle may not always have your best interests at heart and may be looking for a party bud.

Gail is dating a serious drinker. If she expects him to change because she loves him, she is deceiving herself. She can offer love, care and support, but at the end of the day, an addict must realize their own self -worth and decide to drop these unhealthy substances.

People who are addicted to gambling, alcohol, cigarettes, drugs, over-eating or sex will not change easily. You need to decide early if this is the road you want to travel.

I am a planner and like to rise early and get on with my day. I make lists so that I can accomplish a lot each day. I lived with a woman who needed three cups of coffee to start her morning and then an hour to wash and get ready to face the world. It drove me crazy. I have since learned that if someone needs more time to start their day, I can either occupy myself with something else until they are ready, or find someone with a similar schedule to participate in activities that do not interest my partner.

Kurt is a fifty-year-old salesperson who is on the road all day seeing customers. He is overweight, smokes occasionally and does not exercise. His wife Patty is slim, fit and conscious of her diet. Kurt suffered a heart attack five years ago. Patty has stopped trying to help him with advice, because he closed that door. She cooks separately for herself and avoids conversations regarding her diet and exercise routine. Recently, Kurt had another cardiac event and was rushed to the hospital. He required stents for his blocked arteries. Patty supported his recovery, but again, refrained from lecturing or arguing about his lifestyle choices. She hopes this second event will be a louder wake up call for Kurt, and he will begin to make the changes for his own well-being.

Yes, your love for each other may transcend your different lifestyles. If you both share complimentary health and eating habits this question may not be high on your list.

Stan espoused alternative health choices. He visited a naturopath, practiced yoga and read the latest research on natural ways of promoting good health and dealing with illness. Clara, a more traditional lady, followed an eastern-European meat and potatoes diet. This limited their eating out choices since Stan was quite picky about what he ate. In time, they each gave a little and found mutually acceptable restaurants. They recognized they both had things to learn from each other and they continue to grow as a couple.

Constance, a-fifty-year old executive, has smoked for thirty years, starts her day with a diet soda and a cigarette and consumes a bottle of wine each night after work. She met Larry, a construction worker, who had just stopped smoking, did not drink alcohol, and was cutting back on fast food. They came from the same neighborhood and had some mutual friends. They had an easy time together and enjoyed one another's company. Food was not important and they both would eat whatever was available. Since they did not live together and only saw each other on weekends, these differences were not much of an issue. However, over time, as they talked about living together and marriage, Larry was uncomfortable making love with someone who was often drunk and smelled like an ashtray. Constance was frustrated by Larry's free spirit and non-committal attitude. After a couple of years of dating and no progress on lifestyle changes, they parted.

Geoff met Susan and there was an instant physical spark. He had been struggling with his weight and diet for years. She had taken classes on nutrition and was a big influence on his making positive changes to improve his state of health. He fell in love with her positive attitude and healthy lifestyle. He longed for someone to help him stay focused on changing his eating habits and exercise routine. She introduced him to new restaurants, work-out clubs and a circle of active friends. He told me it felt like he was being rescued from a downward spiral of overeating, lack of exercise and negative behavior. He also confessed she liked to date a few guys at a time and did not want to commit to anyone person. This was not what he wanted in a mate. In time, he concluded she was a gift to help in making new choices on health and lifestyle, but a not a love match. Fortunately he said, "I was able to maintain these positive changes and not rely on her to keep me on track."

This reminds me that some people come into our lives for a specific reason, some for a season, and sometimes for a life time.

Do you prefer healthy food or the drive-through?

_____

_____

_____

Circle your compatibility score   1   3   5

Question 11

Chemistry

How much personal space and or time do you need?

How much time do you need for yourself? Are you on the run from the time you open your eyes until your head hits the pillow at the end of the day? When do you take some down time? Is there a period each day or week that you require just for you?

The amount of space and time you require just for yourself will factor into your compatibility with this new person. Can you hang out together and enjoy the silence as you each read, sleep, watch TV or work on separate projects? These are important questions as you settle into a new relationship and determine the amount of time you spend together.

In North America, one adult in seven prefer to live on their own. Are you one of them? The need to be married or share your residence is changing. Yes, many of us still desire the social connection with others and want to live with or be married to someone, but it is not everyone's wish.

Do you enjoy sleeping together or does one of you prefer to sleep alone?

Stan has been married for over thirty years and has an active sexual life with wife, Mia.

He confesses he does not like to hold his wife very long after sex and prefers to sleep in a separate bed. Although other couples enjoy the afterglow of lovemaking and the feelings that follow, Stan and Mia are okay with separating soon after sex.

Ralph, a motorcycle cop, gets up at four a.m. to start his shift patrolling the streets of his town. He told me that he loves his work, but when he gets home, he is spent. He has told his new bride that he needs about an hour to just decompress alone. She understands and leaves him alone as he lets the day go. This clear communication and acceptance works for the health of their marriage.

James divorced after thirty-one years of marriage. He shared that after being alone for two years, he met a lovely lady named Alice. Alice had been living by herself for over twenty years. She was married once and had dated occasionally, but was now happy and comfortable living alone in her own home enjoying her circle of friends. Because James was quite taken with Alice and wanted to see her often and spend nights together, he broached the topic of living together. Alice's aloofness on the matter left James feeling a little unsure of their future. They travelled well together, enjoyed each other's company, but he felt rejected when she pulled away and needed her own space. There was a big discrepancy in how much time they both wanted together and this eventually led to a break up when James found someone else who was open to living together.

Can you easily communicate your need for time alone in a kind and loving manner, or do you just disappear without letting your partner know where you are? Do you want to share your home with another person, or are you happy dating and living in separate places? These are important questions to consider.

Are you an introvert or an extrovert? Do you like planning, socializing and entertaining at home or going out to clubs? If your partner does not like groups and rarely goes out to a community event, restaurant or the theater, but prefers to stay at home, that may present some hurdles for you. Some couples have different friends for different activities and are okay filling their social needs apart.

Jeff works from a home office and does not see anyone all day except the dog and the mailman. His wife Sheila works downtown in a large company with hundreds of employees. She likes going into this large workplace and seeing her colleagues, while Jeff enjoys the quieter time at home. He tells me, at the end of the day, "I need to get out and have some social interaction with friends whereas, Sheila is tired and just wants to relax at home and unwind from her busy day." Some nights, Jeff goes with a friend to a movie or a ballgame that does not include Sheila. On other nights, Jeff and Sheila go out on a date. This works for them as a couple.

Are you someone that wants to constantly be around your partner? Sometimes, distance and time away from each other benefits the relationship and you appreciate each other more because of the temporary separation.

How much personal space and or time do you need?

_____

_____

_____

How much personal space and or time does your partner need?

_____

_____

_____

Circle your compatibility score   1   3   5

Question 12

Chemistry

Is your house messy?

The Dirty socks test.

This may seem like an unimportant question when you are in the throngs of passion with your new partner. Who cares what state you keep your home in? Stay tuned.

Do you like your space to be clean, neat and organized? A drive in your new mate's vehicle or a visit to their home will indicate what time and care they invest in their living space and if you both like the same standards for your homes. Using the back seat of the car as a filing cabinet or trashcan may not appeal to your mate. Leaving dirty socks around the house will stress a partner who likes order and cleanliness.

Cheryl's car was a dumpster with candy wrappers on the back seats, papers scattered everywhere and bags of stuff in the trunk. Sheldon deemed it an unsightly mess. When he visited her home, he found boxes in the middle of the living room, unwashed dishes stacked in the kitchen sink and clothes thrown all over her bedroom. Since he preferred a more orderly living space, this was a warning sign for him foretelling what living with Cheryl might be like.

Yes, he had strong emotions for her, but when he was able to step back and review some other significant differences they had in their spending-saving compatibility, (Pillar Two), he chose not to pursue a relationship with her.

Once the initial trance wears off, it is the small things that can trigger thoughts and feelings that lead to disharmony and stress in relationships. If we do not take note and communicate early the small items that concern or annoy us, they can grow into monsters.

My wife prefers I put my tea cup away after my nightly drink. I sometimes forget, and have assured her I will make an effort. Through civil discussion we are learning how to live together and keep harmony under our roof.

If keeping a tidy home is not a priority for either of you then cleaning up whenever you both decide, or hiring a cleaning lady, may solve the issue.

Frank has been married for over twenty years. I asked him if he was single again what questions he would ask or what he would be observant about with a new love. "That's simple," he said. "I would look for the little things. He called it the dirty socks and dust test. It is the little things that can blossom into big issues. I would look for how she keeps her home and herself," he confessed. He went on that having different cleaning habits is a big issue with his spouse. He likes everything put away once washed or used. She gets to it in her own time and this has been stressful for him.

When I spoke with Gloria she was much more concerned with tidiness than Tim. Before they left for work in the morning, she insisted he wash and put away the dishes rather than rinsing and leaving them in the sink. He asked, "Are you expecting anyone during the day when we are at work?" She replied, "No, but we can't leave the house dirty." This was a routine she had learned from her mother and it ruled her adult life. The bed had to be made properly, the living room tidied and all dishes put out of sight before they went out.

Tim agreed to follow her request since it did not take much effort to place the dishes in the dishwasher after he rinsed them. All relationships require negotiation skills, and he was happy to accommodate this request.

Sam was dating Susan, who lived in an older home built in the 1920's. It had lots of character and a warm feeling to it. However, he noticed dust everywhere, cobwebs on the stairs and the shower was located in an unfinished basement. Susan left pots and boxes in the middle of the kitchen and items piled everywhere. He lived in a more contemporary home and took pride in keeping things clean and stored out of sight. He noticed her car was banged up and full of items making it hard for him to sit comfortably when they travelled together. He felt uncomfortable in these environments and admitted he was not sure if he could live with someone with such different habits.

Is your partner a pack rat? Do they refuse to let go of anything in their home? A storage unit may be a simple solution if you are considering living with this person. Having a garage sale is another great way to free up space and get rid of unneeded stuff. What about donating items you no longer use?

My home office can be messy, but I know where everything is. Since I am the only one using this private space, it is not an issue. The rest of my home and vehicles are clean and orderly. If I have not worn something in two years, I donate it. I tidy up the endless parade of papers coming into my home and religiously compost and recycle daily.

Francis met Jim and felt an immediate sexual pull towards him, she says. They began dating. She discovered he was a natural kind of guy and did not believe in using deordorant or commercial products for cleaning his home. He only used natural soap for washing and vinegar was his main cleanser for his home. Yes, she enjoyed lovemaking with him, but in time his body odor began to repel her. Thankfully, through caring conversations, he was open to finding a natural deodorant and the issue was resolved.

Sharing living space will test your compatibility. If you are comfortable picking up after your partner, fine. If not, then decide early on in the relationship what you are willing to tolerate and communicate your feelings.

It is the little things that often lead to bigger problems. Take the dirty socks test with your partner sooner rather than later.

Is your house messy?

_____

_____

_____

Is your partner's house messy?

_____

_____

_____

Circle your compatibility score   1   3   5

Question 13

Chemistry

Are there any mental or emotional concerns about your partner?

When applying for a job, a bank loan or a volunteer position, the state of our mental health and past performance is evaluated. It is equally valid to consider mental health when considering committing to a long term, personal relationship.

Life can be very difficult and challenging for some, especially if they have a mental illness.

Similar to physical challenges such as diabetes, asthma or heart disease, some forms of mental illness can be managed with medication and therapy. It is important to know if your new love has mental challenges, is seeing a therapist, or is taking medication for certain disorders. When and how they reveal this information is crucial to both of you.

Margaret was a widow who after a couple of years of being single was encouraged to start dating again. She felt like a fish out of water and agreed to try an online introduction. She found a man who seemed very pleasant. Their exchanges revealed that they shared similar life experiences as he was also left alone after his wife died. As they had much in common, they decided to speak on the phone. Within two minutes of their conversation, there was a pause and David said, "I have to tell you something. I am bi-polar." Margaret paused, and then replied, "Isn't that ironic, so am I." They laughed and thought, "Fate has brought us together because we have found the rare mate who would understand us". They began dating, married a few months later and are now enjoying a good life together.

At times we can all feel sad, depressed or challenged, but if these states are the norm for your partner, you need to decide if this is the person you want to be with and if you have the tools to support and manage their issues.

This question may fall under two pillars — Chemistry and Caring: *Can you manage your emotional and mental differences and still maintain your love for each other?*

Does your partner's family have a history of mental illness, drug abuse, alcoholism, or other dysfunctional conditions? Visiting with your partner's family may also provide some insight.

Spending time with someone in various situations reveals mood swings, changes in behavior and can confirm the qualities that attract you to them. You may discover you are both emotionally compatible or that there are issues you were not aware of.

Ben was dating Sylvia, and he shared that after a few months of what he thought was a great relationship, he witnessed a different side of her.

Sylvia ran a home hair styling service and had one client that kept cancelling appointments or not paying her bills. One morning while Ben was waiting for her to finish with this client, he overheard an argument with Sylvia and the customer. Sylvia became very angry and began throwing things and screaming at the client. Ben was shaken by this sudden outburst as the client rushed out of the house remarking she would never return. A few days later while Ben and Sylvia were waiting in line to see a movie, again Sylvia became angry and started yelling at the cashier. These sudden fits of anger concerned Ben. When he tried to discuss this behavior, Sylvia became angry with him too. He recognized that when she was under pressure this was her way of dealing with it. He tried to offer some positive options for handling scenarios that did not go her way, but Sylvia was convinced her anger was justified, and she was perfectly okay telling people off. This soured Ben's interest in pursuing a future with her.

How do you or your partner handle stress? Does one suppress their feelings, drink too much or lash out, while the other focuses on how to resolve the obstacle with calm and rational thinking? Learning how you both deal with change, challenge and fear will provide a more resourceful toolbox to communicate, negotiate and work together.

Are there any emotional or mental concerns you have about your partner?

_____

_____

_____

Circle your compatibility score   1   3   5

Question 14

Chemistry

Are you a dreamer or achiever?

"I want to, but ..."

This question may provide you with some understanding of your partner's level of commitment and ability to fulfill promises and achieve their goals. Do they jump from task to task and quit early — never really getting much completed? Or, can they follow a plan, make a commitment and achieve what they want to.

Do you have completion chemistry with them? Are you a sprinter and your new love is a marathon achiever? Knowing your potential mate's rhythm and pace when it comes to completing tasks and fulfilling promises will provide you with important information in deciding if you can work and live together. A simple goal of keeping the house clean, taking the car for a wash, paying a bill on time or remembering your important social date are clues to a future together.

Some people are very content with a regular routine with their job, home, and family. They get ruffled if anything changes, or they are asked to think outside their comfort zone. They are happy to follow when someone else initiates a project, but do not hold your breath waiting for them to take the lead. Some people would rather die than change — and often do.

Petra, who has been married to Bill for twelve years, loves to travel overseas to developing countries. Bill has no interest in going anywhere without a flush toilet and clean water. Petra researches, plans and executes two trips a year with friends and relishes her adventures. It is easy for her to imagine a project and complete it. Bill is more laid back and finishes projects whenever he can. Over time, they have learned to accept these differences and it works for them.

Are you the boss or the worker, the leader or the follower? The twenty/eighty rule applies in most relationships whether in the workplace, community, or love. It states that twenty percent of people perform eighty percent or the work and reap eighty percent of the rewards. Have you noticed in your relationships there is usually one who carries more of the load be it financial, social, sexual or domestic? Does the saying, "If you want something accomplished, give it to a busy person" ring true in your relationship? Are you the one making most of the effort to maintain the health and vibrancy of your union? Are you okay being the planner and completer of tasks? Does your partner share your desire to achieve and advance?

Does your partner deliver on promises and finish projects? Sometimes life happens and we get sidetracked, but be aware if repeated excuses are a consistent pattern with your new love. Whether the commitment is small for example, "I will call in an hour," or "I will ask my financial advisor to get the answer to your question," or a larger one like, "I am going to take a class to advance my career," you need dependability in a love match.

Kevin told me he was attracted to women who can set a goal and go for it. He gave the example of Jennifer, a lady he was considering moving in with. She had been commenting for months about changing the color of the walls in her apartment and buy some new furniture, yet had made little effort to look at paint options, go to the hardware store, browse the furniture websites or stores, or set a date to begin the updating of her home. Kevin repeatedly offered to help her, but there was always an excuse. He began to notice a pattern in her life about all the things she wanted to change, but rarely made the effort to begin. He admitted, "I don't have much patience for those caught in the valley of excuses." He realized Jennifer had an inability to make decisions and act on them.

If you are both conservative in your goals and lifestyles and are comfortable with what you have, that may work perfectly for you. However, if you have the desire to live a more dynamic life and make every moment an opportunity to learn and grow as much as you can, it will be very helpful to have a partner who dances at the same speed.

Why wait for New Year's to set resolutions?

Is there chemistry between you and how you both create and realize your dreams?

Are you a dreamer or achiever?

_____

_____

_____

Is your partner a dreamer or achiever?

_____

_____

_____

| Circle your compatibility score | 1 | 3 | 5 |

Question 15

Chemistry

Should we live together before marriage?

During the dating phase of a new relationship you may see each other a couple of times a week, spend a weekend or take a short vacation together. But living in the same house full time is a very different experience. Do not be fooled or convinced by the best behavior you witness during short social activities.

I spent five days on my first date with the woman I eventually married – a unique and insightful experience. She was vacationing in a city far from home and after corresponding for a few weeks by phone and e-mail I decided to visit her at her summer place. She welcomed me with no obligation to stay more than a day, but we hit it off and the next five days together were extremely helpful in getting to know each other quickly. We shared making meals, had many discussions on a variety of topics and spent every hour together. If I had not liked her immediately, I would have been on my way in a few hours. We repeated another seven-day second date, as we like to call it, a few weeks later and built on our earlier experience. It felt like homecoming week and we fell into a very comfortable and natural groove together. If you are serious about finding a life partner, I recommend this method of discovery. Our twelve days together felt like a trial living arrangement and provided us a preview of what our future would hold. We talked about money, careers, families, childhood, friends and lifestyles. We realized we had similar views on life, goals and were very compatible in communicating to each other.

Are you both willing to share household chores, expenses and the effort needed to make social time with family and friends? Besides sharing a bed together, can you happily share yard work, making meals, paying bills or raising kids?

Rita, a couple's coach, suggested new partners should go on a week-long ship cruise together. She told me she believes it's a quick way to discover many things about each other confined to the same vessel 24/7. Camping over a weekend was another suggestion that Phil, a recently single friend encouraged. "It's a great opportunity to see first if you both enjoy the outdoors, and how you will work together outside your regular comfort zone"

Some long-time married couples I spoke to say you should live together a minimum of a year before getting married. "It takes time and different challenges to see if you are compatible on most things," stated Frank and Marion, a couple married for twenty-two years. If you recall earlier in the book, I interviewed a manager of a store about how she knows when she is in love and she replied, "Until we have faced some adversity together, I have no idea if I love someone or if they truly love me".

There are always exceptions to the living together recommendation and some couples did not need this period before marriage to know they had something special and very compatible. The five pillars lined up and they just knew it would work. Bob and Barbara met, and after just three weeks, married and have been together over forty years.

There is also a growing trend of couples that decide to live together and have no desire to marry. Some even have children together and that works for them. Regardless, their compatible pillars obviously lined up.

Reviewing the other questions in this book to help determine if your lives are truly compatible beyond the initial trance state will help you decide if you want to take the first step of living together or if you are ready to take your relationship straight to marriage.

Should we live together before getting married?

_____

_____

_____

Circle your compatibility score   1   3   5

Question 16

Chemistry

Whom do you dislike?

"What are your prejudices and concerns?"

"I'm black; she's white; our kids are yellow, and who cares?" In an ideal world that may be the anthem, but most of us bring some prejudicial baggage to our relationships.

Some people have difficulty accepting other races, cultures, religions, sexual orientations and those with challenges.. If you are more accepting of others while your mate expresses negative opinions about individuals or groups, you may experience more conflict than you signed up for.

How do your beliefs and prejudices affect your associations with friends and family? If your family and friends are of a different ethnic or racial group and your mate has fears or is closed-minded about them, where does that leave you?

Rachel, who was dating Phil, thought he might be the one until they went to a party with some of her college friends. Phil discovered she had gay and lesbian friends. He was very uncomfortable with this crowd and voiced his concerns on the way home. She was surprised and realized he had negative views of other minorities too. She tried to explore the source of his prejudice and discovered he had limited experience with gay people or those from eastern Asia. He shared that a relative had a bad experience with a gay man and this one incident had colored his views. She realized in one evening they were on very different pages and she backed away.

"Never discuss religion or politics" may be wise when first talking with strangers, but it is an out-dated adage when it involves a lover. If you plan on spending your life with this person, it is vital that you feel free to express, share, and hopefully participate with them in your social, religious and political interests.

I dated someone who was more right-sided politically than I am. We were able to joke and share our ideas with respect. Neither of us was trying to convince or change the other, we simply voiced our opinions. The ideal goal between couples is a willingness to have a discussion and not a debate, on topics that are sensitive to one or the other.

If you plan on having children with this person it is wise to clearly understand their thoughts and feelings about faith, schools, parenting, and acceptance of other ethnicities.

Most bigotry and racism stems from a lack of exposure to, or experience with, other cultures. We sometimes adopt the beliefs of our elders without personal experience with people from other cultures, or even neighborhoods in our own town.

Overbearing parents who threaten us in ways that can be very persuasive, fearful and in some instances violent, can strengthen our prejudices. We have read and heard about parents killing their children because the offspring did not share their cultural or religious beliefs.

Brad and Polly had a serious disagreement about a proposed home in their neighborhood for adults with mental challenges. Polly thought it was wonderful that the community was trying to integrate the residents into a normal neighborhood. Brad wanted nothing to do with it and had strong opposition to this type of housing in his backyard. His wife was stunned by his views.

I had been invited to a barbecue in a small town with a girlfriend. I engaged in casual conversation with a young man who sat opposite me while munching on a burger. Within five minutes, he made some rude comments about black people, Jews, and gays. I had an instinctual response to rip his head off; however, I took a breath and decided to use this as an opportunity. I asked him how many black friends he had and he quickly responded, "None." I continued with the same question about Jewish people, and again, he had no experience with people of the Hebrew faith. I said, "So your strong beliefs about them are based on what?" He paused, thought and then replied, "I guess, I'm not sure." I proceeded to ask him about his interaction with anyone who was gay. He quickly shot back, "No way, I hate them." I continued, "So you have no personal experience with any of the people you have just insulted?" He stopped again, reflected and then admitted, he had no exposure or experience with any of these groups and was just repeating what his family and friends echoed throughout his years. I walked away and wondered if living in a small community where everyone looks the same contributes to this sense of separation, misperception, and fear of others. I asked my girlfriend on the way back to the city if she had any strong prejudices against any ethnic or cultural groups. Thankfully, she did not.

What kind of world did your partner grow up in? Were they limited in their interaction with people of different cultures or social class? I found a difference in those raised in small towns versus an urban upbringing. Larger cities offer exposure to a multitude of ethnicities and provide the opportunity to meet and engage people from different backgrounds. This adds to our understanding and acceptance of the differences we encounter in others. Does your partner have the same history as you of living, studying, and working with people who are different from them?

Before judging others, I suggest you make a list of the individuals or groups you dislike. How has your family influenced your choices of lovers and friends? It is easy to fool ourselves into thinking we are open-minded and accepting of everyone, but it takes confidence and trust to share a bias. We all carry opinions and preferences with who and what we are comfortable with.

Whom do you dislike?

_____

_____

_____

Whom does your partner dislike?

_____

_____

_____

Circle your compatibility score 1 3 5

Question 17

Chemistry

How important are your political stripes?

"Do you lean right, left or are you stuck in the middle?"

Some people believe you should not discuss politics or religion. I believe if you have an open mind and are respectful of others' points of view, you can have an intelligent conversation and learn a lot about someone at the same time.

If you have a strong political affiliation and insist your partner shares your views, that may limit the pool of potential mates, but if this is a top requirement, it will also make it easier to find a potential partner. However, if you fall in love with someone who holds different political ideas than you, it may provide new opportunity for growth and discussion.

Gail, a Republican, was quick to state her position on issues. She told me she was an old-school conservative who admired her party's legacy. She met liberal-minded Frank and teased him for being a tree-hugging Democrat. They laughed about their differences and shared their ideas and views. By doing this it enhanced their bond because the foundation of their relationship was based on openness and acceptance — not control and demands.

Susan shared with me that she felt compelled to go to political rallies and express her views at community events. She was passionate about her beliefs and could not fathom being with a partner who did not share her convictions. Devon had very strong personal views about politics, but preferred to voice his opinions more privately and had no desire to march, protest, or sign petitions. They realized at an early stage they were on very different pages and decided to be just friends.

Your political views may have a dramatic effect on how you worship God, raise children, participate in your community, and even your choice of friends.

In a class I attended called, "Is there room for civil discourse in the public square?", one of the principal questions asked was, "Are you willing to have a dialogue versus a debate?". If your intent is to force your political beliefs down your partner's throat and convince them that your point of view is correct, you may find yourself debating alone.

Will your political stripes overshadow the other four pillars of compatibility? How willing are you to accept someone else's point of view and still focus on the many positive qualities that attract you to this person?"

How important are your political stripes?

_____

_____

_____

How important are your partner's political stripes?

_____

_____

_____

| Circle your compatibility score | 1 | 3 | 5 |

Question 18

Chemistry

Do you recognize your parents in your partner?

"How far did the apple fall from the tree?"

Do you see qualities, attitudes, and behaviors in your partner that your own parents share? Some believe we marry one of our parent's personalities.

Whether one or two parents raise us in a happy or stressful home plays a huge role in how we view and behave with our lover. What we observed and experienced with our parents is imprinted on us. Their behaviors, attitudes, and beliefs have influenced how we seek, recognize, and interact with a partner. The qualities we expect or desire in a mate originate from our formative years as we watched how the adults in our life, especially our primary caregivers, treated each other and dealt with life's challenges. This includes both positive and abusive experiences.

Have you ever stopped to reflect on how similar your partner may be to your father or mother? Are there characteristics they possess that remind you of your family growing up and the relationships you had with one or both of your parents?

Harville Henricks, the well know relationship author, has many interesting and helpful ideas about what attracts us to each other.

Joe described to me that he grew up in a traditional Greek home where his Mom did all the work inside the home while his Dad worked outside the house. Joe expected his wife would look after the house, cook, raise the kids, and make a nice home. When his new girlfriend shared she was not in a rush for kids, enjoyed her career and had plotted her course to climb the corporate ladder, Joe admitted he was taken aback.

Did your parents share responsibilities in your home? Did both parents work outside the house? Did they struggle to pay the bills and provide for all your needs? Were your parents openly affectionate or did you observe a lack of passion? Did they argue often or was anger or disagreement suppressed?

After dating my first girlfriend in college for a few months, she invited me to a family dinner. I grew up in a calm home where we rarely raised our voices or debated and arguments were quickly extinguished. When I arrived at her parents' home, they welcomed me. When we sat down to dinner, the circus began. The tone and volume of her parents' and siblings' conversation shocked me. I had not witnessed such a loud exchange among family members before, and I did not know where to look or whom to speak to first. Her Dad seemed very angry and was snapping at her Mom, shouting above the other kids at the table. I was exhausted at the end of the evening and couldn't wait to run out the front door.

I later learned that her Dad was a holocaust survivor and had witnessed the murder of his parents and siblings in the concentration camps. He had been liberated as a teen and had come to North America alone and unable to speak English to start a new life. I thought it was amazing that he was able to function, let alone, marry and raise five kids.

As my relationship continued with his daughter, it was still very hard for me to handle her outbursts of anger and her raised voice when we had a disagreement. The apple did not fall far from her parents' tree. I eventually realized I could not live with someone like this. Although my parents had some cultural similarities to hers, their manner of communication repelled me.

I have an acquaintance Rinder, who is a Sikh. He emigrated from India, built a business and after a few years decided it was time for a wife. His family back in India arranged for him to meet a local girl, whom he eventually met, married and brought to North America. She quickly engaged in her new life and became a dental assistant and started earning a nice living. They had two children together and were living the western lifestyle, but he was unhappy. I asked what the issue was and he replied, "I do not want her to be like modern women here. I want an Indian wife who will stay at home and look after the children." He was looking for his mother in a wife and was disappointed when his spouse adopted the life he introduced her to.

Did your parents project their fears and insecurities onto you regarding money, caring, communication and commitment? Have you found a partner who faces the same issues? Did you learn about respect, honor and affection from your folks? Whether healthy or dysfunctional, we inherit qualities from our parents that we sometimes project onto lovers.

I chatted with Diane at an author's festival and she shared she has been married for 32 years. I asked her what the secret was and she quickly responded, "we are psychology compatible". She went on to say that she learned early in her marriage she was attracted to the qualities in her husband she felt she was lacking in, and when the conflict began because of their differences she recognized what was happening. Through hard work and some counseling they found ways to be together and deal with these sore areas. She continued, "most couples I know jump ship when they realize how different they are and might find a better way in their second or third marriages".

It is a valuable exercise to explore your partner's relationship with their parents and to observe the similarities that they have adopted. It may provide clues about who they are and what your life will be like with them.

Do you recognize your parents in your partner?

_____

_____

_____

Circle your compatibility score   1   3   5

Chemistry compatibility Rating Review

You have now completed all the Chemistry pillar questions.

Total the number of #1s = little in common, #3s = some things in common and #5s = very compatible.

1 ___   3 ___   5 ___

You have now reviewed 18 questions. Congratulations.

Pillar Two: Cash

Question 19

Cash

How easy is it to talk about finances?

This is probably the most important pillar to explore early in a relationship. With the pressures of modern living and the expenses we all incur, you need to know sooner rather than later what your new love's ideas, habits, history, and future plans are for money. At some point, if this relationship continues with talks of living together or marriage, money will be THE ELEPHANT in the room that needs careful attention and discussion.

If a woman earns more than the man, does this change the dynamic of the relationship? As a man, are you okay with earning less than your partner? If one partner decides not to work, can the other afford to support both of you?

Conversely, does a woman want to know she will be looked after? On a primal level, does she look to the man as her protector, provider and prince?

Lucas, a friend of mine, who has been with his partner for over twenty years, attended a party at my house. He noticed many of the guests were professional singles.

"Your friends are freaks," he said.

"Freaks? What do you mean," I asked.

"Your friends don't need anyone. They are successful and independent. Why would they need a partner?" He then said, "Regardless of how much money a woman makes or how independent she appears, they all want a man to look after, provide for and protect them." Is this true, I wondered? After decades of women fighting for equal rights, salary parity and careers, do some women still have the desire or instinct to be cared for and protected?

Does one of you owe a lot of money? Are you challenged to manage your spending habits and expenses? How does this affect your relationship now? How will this affect your relationship in the future together? Will this debt limit your lifestyle, ability to travel, entertainment choices, and your own purchases? Is there an expectation that your partner will bail you out?

Review your current money interactions. Does one of you pay for most of your social activities? Is there a balance between who pays for what and how you handle expenses. This may be a sign of things to come.

If you live together or marry, is there an expectation that one will pay for most of your shared expenses? Will there be a joint bank account for household costs? Will one of you assume the role of paying the bills each month from your joint account? How will you handle the assets earned before you ever met? Is a pre-nuptial agreement needed? Will you move into one person's home or the other, or will you rent or buy a new house together?

If one or both of you have children, how will the daily living costs be handled?

Take note of your partner's plans and promises because sometimes when the money picture changes so do their obligations.

Talking to different couples made it clear: Money is one critical subject few couples wanted to discuss. It was awkward for them to discuss in front of each other. It poked at a sensitive area. For couples
that were new to their relationship, it risked waking them from the
trance of romance. Even though it was a difficult topic, all agreed a
healthy discussion about money matters was important before marriage. If someone is important enough to be your partner in a relationship, it is important to have the awareness, even courage, to have
a conversation about finances.

How easy is it to talk about finances?

_____

_____

_____

Circle your compatibility score   1   3   5

Question 20

Cash

Who pays for what and when?

This is one of those challenging questions about money that can be tricky to discuss early in a new relationship. The answers you both share at the appropriate time will be most revealing.

Since money issues can be the greatest source of relationship hell, it is wise to find out early what your habits, beliefs, and behaviors are regarding money.

How you spend, save, and use money will provide great insight into your compatibility. Your level of generosity, saving or spending might differ dramatically from that of your new love. The simple act of tipping generously for good service will reveal important insights about your partner's attitude about money.

Joel dated Lindsay a few times. He told me that she forgot to bring cash or a debit card and rarely offered to treat him. "If I ask someone out," he explained, "I expect to pay for that date and even the first few outings, but if we continue to see each other, I think it is reasonable that we find a way to share expenses." He was disappointed that she didn't think enough of him to make an effort. He explained that if she couldn't afford some of the places they went she could find other options such as, find an inexpensive diner, cook a meal or make dessert, or pack a picnic basket for lunch in the park.

Michele's story was similar. For several months, she dated Brad. They had good conversations that eventually developed into an intimate relationship. From her post-relationship perspective, she admitted it was clear to her that she fell into a trance. She convinced herself she was in love despite significant signs of trouble. One day while visiting his home, it occurred to her that he had never offered her a cup of coffee or made her a sandwich, let alone treated her to a restaurant meal. She gently requested, "Hey, it would be really nice if you made me a meal sometime." He replied, "I don't cook but you are welcome to my fridge. Feel free to make yourself something." Michele told me that Brad had missed the point. She was asking for a sign of his consideration for her.

Although Michele was shaken briefly from the trance, she fooled herself into thinking, "Well, that's okay; he treats me nicely in other ways." A week later, she was cast in a local community theater production. To her surprise, Brad had no interest in seeing the production.

This was the nudge she needed to realize she had fallen back into the trance. She realized for the past three months she took all the initiative. When he visited her home, she treated him with small gifts, cooked for him and showed a sincere interest in his life. When they went out, most of the time she paid. Finally, it dawned on her that Brad was more interested in taking than giving.

"Who do you think should pay when we go out?" She asked him.

"You make more money than I do. You should." This snapped her completely free of the trance she had fallen into.

You may believe if one person earns more, they can afford to pay for more. However, a habit of one-sided payment, without reciprocation, can lead to resentment. Joel and Michele showed how that resentment could build up and spill over into other areas of the relationship. If this is a concern for you, take some time and have a discussion with your mate.

Identifying your combined disposable income together will help determine your lifestyle together. Clearly, if one has expenses associated with kids and a house and the other does not, this will likely limit disposable income in addition to social activities, travel plans and other outings.

This was the case with Leon. Semi-retired and childless, Leon finally had the flexibility to buy a recreational vehicle and travel south during the winter months. On his travels, he met Sherri. She was recently divorced, unemployed and looking for work and she had two teenagers living at home. Leon and Sherri began a relationship. He visited her every few weeks or they would meet somewhere to spend time together. He had strong feelings for her. The relationship suited his lifestyle. However, Sherri was struggling with financial pressures while searching for a job. She did not have the financial flexibility to match Leon's lifestyle. Leon tells me that over time, Sherri began to resent his freedom. They were on two very different pages. In time, they realized this arrangement was too difficult and they decided to go their separate ways.

If you find you can no longer do the things you are accustomed to enjoying or are paying for almost everything, eventually, you may feel short-changed. If however, you have no issues about paying for everything and sharing your lifestyle, it may work out just fine.

Gary and Rachel are neighbors and socialize often. Rachel had romantic feelings for Gary, but he seemed content just to be friends. Whenever they went to a restaurant or a movie, he insisted they share the bill to the penny. Sometimes this became tedious and frustrating for Rachel because she felt it was no big deal to pay an extra dollar or two for such small items. "No, no," he insisted, "We share the cost of everything right down the middle." "Life is too short for such time-consuming, small mindedness," she shared with me. She also noticed that Gary was quite stubborn and would argue excessively to make a point or hold his view on insignificant topics. Again, Rachel thought, "I would rather be happy than right all the time." She awoke from her fantasy and realized a romantic relationship with him would be futile. She accepted his position on sharing expenses and they remain friends.

How does your potential mate handle their finances? Are they always in debt and struggling to meet their monthly expenses? Are they unable to enjoy an evening on the town or a weekend getaway? If you can easily afford these pleasures and they cannot, eventually, you may resent carrying the wallet, and they may begin to feel inferior or dependent for not being able contributing equally.

Do you both have future plans for a vacation home, children's educational needs, investments, and retirement? These big-ticket items affect the nature of your social time together. If you choose to live together, what type of lifestyle will you enjoy?

If one of you became ill and lost their job, is the other willing and able to cover the costs until recovery? Have you made contingency plans for a sudden change in cash flow?

Are you willing to explore disability and life insurance options with your partner? More importantly, how easy is it to discuss these issues in an open and honest exchange?

Rick, who has been married three times, shared with me that even now in his seventies, he feels uncomfortable discussing money matters with the wonderful woman he is currently dating. His last divorce resulted in his ex-wife receiving a large portion of his retirement money. He and his new girlfriend share homes and winter down south together. If their relationship proceeds to talks of marriage, he told me that he realized that he would have to address money, maybe even a pre-nuptial agreement.

Is there a need to discuss a pre-nup agreement so there is no guessing or misunderstanding about the resolution of money matters if the relationship sours or someone dies? Some think this is putting a cloud over the joy of your new love. To that I say, "Santa Clause and the Tooth Fairy can offer you counseling if your joyous state changes to the reality of day-to-day life that leads to separation or divorce." Property ownership, bank accounts, retirement accounts, and insurance are not traditionally romantic topics. Blended families further complicate finances.

A pre-nup is another aspect of identifying up-front who/what pays for what.

What are you each bringing to the union? Is there equal property value, equal contributions to a new home, or is there a large difference in your incomes, careers, and financial status? These are important questions that need to be asked and answered before you fall deeper into emotional and financial entanglement.

How will you handle your bank accounts? Numerous couples shared that a joint account works well for common household expenses while each person retains a separate personal account to provide a level of financial independence and autonomy.

Marty fell in love with a woman with a shady past. Gwen was very attractive and turned him on in a variety of ways. She told him after declaring bankruptcy, she moved across the country to live with a man who provided a lavish life for her. She did not have to work. When that live-in arrangement ended, she was bitter, broke, and desperate to find a place to land. Marty had a home, a business, and financial security. He thought they could make a life together.

In his trance, he was blind to her patterns with money and men. He invited her into his world and began providing for her. Family and friends warned him of her motives. Because of his trance, he resented their comments.

In hindsight, he realized his family and friends' interference showed that they cared. He did not resent paying for all the household expenses with Gwen, but eventually he grew to resent her attitude of entitlement, her lack of appreciation and respect for him. As Marty tried to discuss how finances affected their relationship, she protested that it was Marty who had the money issues and not her. After much hardship, Marty was able to dislodge her from his home.

Do you believe it is important that each partner is financially stable, or that one spouse should be financially responsible for the other?

Unless you discuss your expectations it can cause division and big surprises down the road.

For example, Terry and Michael, a young couple, divorced after only two years of marriage. Michael was proud to be a good provider for his wife. He worked in a successful family business, which provided a big house, cars, and all the other material trappings. Michael was always at work or at his parents' home satisfying the family's demands. For Terry, the successful family business resulted in her in-laws always being around, meddling in her marriage. She would have traded a simpler home for more time with Michael. No amount of money would bring her the closeness she longed for with her husband. Eventually, she walked away from this life. In talking to Terry, it was clear that money was not her number one priority in their relationship.

Most of the people I interviewed for this book agreed that money could be a difficult subject. Most didn't discuss money matters before getting into a long-term relationship. They waited until they had to set up household finances or, worse, when it became a problem in the relationship. Everyone agreed it was important to talk about money at the beginning of the relationship – and to keep the dialogue going.

Who pays for what and when?

_____

_____

_____

Circle your compatibility score   1   3   5

Question 21

Cash

Can you manage financially without your partner's income?

Can you manage financially without your partner's income? This is a pivotal question within the pillar of compatibility marked CASH. Finances are one of the most common challenges in sustaining relationships. Money issues are often the root of disappointment and anger towards a partner. Resentment can be expressed very directly or covertly by a change in behavior towards your partner such as withholding affection, becoming aloof, or not communicating.

If one of the primary reasons you have interest in someone is the lifestyle they provide, this may be a short-term fix instead of an investment in a lifelong relationship.

Ideally, if both parties are financially stable and independent with similar income levels and assets, they can create an even better life by combining resources. However, when someone is eager to jump into your world because they are struggling, cannot manage their own financial affairs, or are broke, be cautious about being a financial life raft until you have spent a lot of time together. Ensure you have discussed your money matters with them. If necessary, consider taking steps to protect assets.

Kevin dated a woman with a teenage daughter at home who worked three jobs and struggled to keep food in the fridge. After a few months, he was in love with her, so he broached the topic of marriage. Vera clearly stated, "If we were to marry, I would expect you as the head of the house to pay for everything." Kevin was dumbstruck. He wondered what decade she was living in. He told me his expectation was for her to contribute to the household in addition to being the primary support for her own daughter. He was grateful to have this conversation early and he decided this was not what he wanted and ended the relationship.

If you are both young, just getting started in your careers and/or living at home, this is an opportune time to explore what your future plans are and what the money dance is between you. How do you handle social activity expenses, gifts, and vacations? You can often see signs of a person's attitudes about money regardless of what stage they are at in the asset-building process. The saying, "Money doesn't change a person; it makes them more of who they are," is something to observe.

Someone who spends a lot more than they earn or have is signaling trouble ahead.

Dave worked hard as a project manager for a grocery chain. His stay-at-home wife was busy with two young kids. Each month her credit cards were maxed out and Dave feared if he got her another card she would simply run that one up to the limit too. He secretly asked his folks for a loan to offset the big expenses, then felt guilty about keeping the secret from his wife. Dave wondered if she had a pattern of overspending before they were married. Was that pattern always there or started when they had children?

Marie met Doug on a summer holiday and they began dating and sharing some wonderful outings. Doug lived in another state and returned home very happy that he had met Marie. Marie called a couple of days after Doug returned to his home to thank him for a wonderful few days and to ask if how they shared expenses was okay with him. Doug replied, "You are the first person who has ever considered asking me that, thank you." He knew he had met someone who was responsible and caring. They continued their correspondence, eventually evolving into a long-term relationship.

Keep in mind that generosity can be expressed in many ways and not always monetarily. If someone does not have your income or cash flow, they can demonstrate their care and consideration by treating you to home-cooked meals, small gifts, or low-cost social outings.

Think about long-term plans together. How will you manage your money? Is one partner better at tracking and paying bills, investing, and budgeting? If you are okay with one person taking on that role and you focus on other strengths that might work well.

Some couples prefer to have a joint banking account for common expenses and maintain separate personal accounts for their own savings and investments. Other teams agree to pool all their monies together. There is no right way, but money matters require discussion before you venture too far into your life together. Discussing who will work full-time or part-time or who will stay at home to raise the kids will determine your budget and your lifestyle.

Money matters can be one of the scariest topics for most people involved in a romantic relationship. Take a deep breath and broach the subject of money if you are falling for someone and have dreams of living together and/or marrying them.

Can you manage financially without your partner's income?

_____

_____

_____

Circle your compatibility score   1   3   5

Question 22

Cash

How do you define success?

"Contentment or toys?"

If your definition of a successful lifestyle does not align with your partner's, you can anticipate some difficulties.

Do you crave the biggest house on the street, the newest cars, the best schools for your kids and the latest gadgets and toys? Can you afford these things? If so, you are lucky to be able to have what you want. Conversely, are you happy with what you have and can afford? If so, you are lucky to want what you have.

If you both are in the same income bracket and accustomed to the same lifestyle, then that may be the start to a good match.

It may be helpful to ask your new love, "What does success mean to you?" Greg realized this with Susan. After eight months of dating, he proposed to her. When he began the search for an engagement ring, he was overwhelmed by the many options available. Some sales clerks told him that a woman expected an engagement ring to cost between 3 and 4 months salary as a reflection of how much a man loves her. He was shocked and disappointed with this attitude.

For Greg, an engagement ring, whether modest or expensive, was a symbol of his level of commitment to Susan. He wondered if Susan was more interested in a large display on her finger to showcase to the world, or his serious desire to share his life with her. Fortunately, she wanted a simple ring and shared his belief that the ring symbolized their love and commitment to each other.

Your background may affect your definition of success. Are you accustomed to status and wealth or do you come from a working class family? Was education your most important goal motivating you to achieve financially? Do you expect your partner to have the same academic accomplishments as you? Does your partner earn more or less money than you? Does any of this matter to you?

Do you share the same goals as your partner?

Richard had a very close childhood friend, Mark. After finishing high school, Richard bounced from job to job with no goal or direction and struggled to earn a good living. He never married. In contrast, Mark went on to get a Ph.D. He is now married with two children.

Richard finds it hard to understand why his best boyhood friend does not invest much time hanging out with him. Their lifestyles, interests and incomes as adults are so vastly different that they have little in common. Yes, they have great childhood memories, but Richard seems stuck in that earlier time period, whereas, Mark is living a different life with his family and a rewarding profession. It is true that they could still find common ground to enjoy each other's company, but neither is willing to make that effort.

Sometimes, our past is exactly that – our past. Does your new love drift along living day to day? Does your new love have goals or dreams? Has you new love busted their butt studying, advancing a career, and creating financial stability? How do you compare your goals and dreams? These are differences that may become challenges down the road. If you are accepting of each other's goals and dreams for careers, life paths, and income levels then it may well work for you as it did for Joanne and Ricardo

Joanne told me that she is a superintendent for a large school district, and earns a larger salary than her husband Ricardo, who works for the city sanitation department. Each has a different circle of colleagues. Early in their relationship, they recognized and accepted their different career paths. They have created a marriage with mutual friends, shared interests, and continue to support each other's success with their career paths.

Personal qualities may be the most important consideration in creating a sacred union. A person who is big-hearted, kind, generous, witty, affectionate, and who treats you and others with respect may be what you need to sustain a happy and healthy relationship. If so, the financial aspects of the relationship may be one of the pillars you can negotiate together.

Do you place strict demands on yourself to achieve success? Is your partner more laid back, allowing life to unfold as it does? Does this provide balance or drive you crazy?

One definition of success I like says, "If where you are and where you want to be are the same place, then you are successful." Discussing where you both are and where you want to be together will define what success means to you. Using the five pillars of compatibility in this discussion will help charter your present course and the road ahead.

If you are not in the same place, that is okay, provided you both acknowledge you have the desire and ability to work together towards some common goals.

It may take time and experience together to reveal if you are on the same path, but recognizing your differences, strengths, common goals and sharing your image of success, will prove to be fruitful.

How do you define success?

_____

_____

_____

How does your partner define success?

_____

_____

_____

Circle your compatibility score   1   3   5

Cash Compatibility Rating Review

You have now completed all the Cash pillar questions.

Total the number of #1s = little in common, #3s = some things in common and #5s = very compatible.

1 ___ 3 ___ 5 ___

You have now reviewed 22 questions. Congratulations.

Pillar Three: Communication

Question 23

Communication

What kind of communicator are you?

In a new relationship, we know little about our partner's preferences, patterns or ways of communicating, and it takes some time to discover them. It is a good idea to explore these areas early to make a conscious assessment of whom you are opening your heart to before the cloud of sexual attraction confuses you.

Gary Chapman, author of "Love Languages," writes extensively about different communication styles, and makes a critical point in saying that not knowing your lover's preferred language can lead to major disappointment, frustration, and ultimately separation. If you like to hear daily words of love, appreciation and affection from your partner, it can be frustrating if your partner, rather than expressing feelings in words, silently demonstrates love in actions by fixing things around the home, helping with chores or planting a garden. If you are not comfortable dealing with differences in a kind, open and consistent manner, you may have some landmines awaiting you. In the early weeks or months of a relationship, we likely are still in that trance state. We spend time thinking about this new person. We like calling, sending e-mails and texts, surprising them with gifts and cards, being playful, and just having fun as we get to know each other. What happens when differences arise? Are we willing to be honest and communicate our thoughts and feelings or do we back away from serious discussion for fear of breaking the trance?

Frank saw differences in communication styles with his girlfriend Toni. He liked to call her first thing each morning to say good morning. Eventually, he noticed that Toni rarely called him at any time. When he told her that he really liked hearing her voice, she replied simply, "I prefer to text." He found this a little impersonal for his needs. Later, he again tried to convey his desire to hear her voice. This fell on deaf ears. It was the first of several differences that he found to be cool, putting distance between them in their relationship. Eventually, Frank realized that he preferred someone who was more affectionate and verbal, and who would take time during the day to talk to him, if only for a few minutes.

Identifying your preferences and sharing them, respectfully, with someone new allows the opportunity to learn about each other on a deeper level. Maybe you enjoy frequent texts and emails to share details throughout the day. Maybe you enjoy speaking on the phone once a day. Maybe you want to talk only when you have something on your mind. Sometimes, your communication styles will align. Other times, you will need to express the level and method of communication that you prefer and find a common ground.

I lived with someone who rarely offered any ideas about activities we could share. When I asked, "What do you want to do today?" She would say, "I'm fine with whatever you want." Initially, in the trace, I found her flexible and easy going. But after a few months, I realized her response was an indicator that she wanted me to do all the planning.

When I spent time with Sue and Bill, it was clear that Sue was a high energy "Chatty Cathy," while Bill was an easy-going, laid-back guy.

They had been married just over a year. During my time with them, I noticed that anytime a topic came up that he did not want to discuss he would say the same thing, "Yes, we can talk about that later." When I had a chance to speak with him privately, I asked about this response. He said his wife was a high-energy woman, and he learned if he waited a while, they could resolve issues easier. This worked for them. If there were an important matter that needed addressing, they would discuss it privately or let it go.

Charlotte also developed a communication technique with her husband. Charlotte told me,, "I tell him exactly what I want. For example, I do not assume he will guess what gift I want on my birthday or anniversary. I'll be as specific as possible." She learned early in their relationship, that her husband, a scientist and academic, did not grasp subtle communication. When he asked what she wanted for Christmas, she put the catalogue on his desk, marked the page and noted her preferred color and correct size. Although this method may not be for everyone, it worked for them.

Some people you will meet have been raised to avoid sharing their feelings. Many people choose to place other's feelings ahead of their own and become people pleasers rarely stating their wants or asking for what makes them happy.

Knowing what type of communicator you are will help you better understand and express your wants to your partner. Learning about their communication preferences will do the same for you.

What kind of communicator are you?

What kind of communicator is your partner?

_____

_____

_____

Circle your compatibility score   1   3   5

Question 24

Communication

Are you a curious George/ Georgette?

"I wonder who.....?"

How curious are you about life? Do you like to question things? Do you wonder about how things work or why people behave as they do? Do you ponder the bigger questions of life: Why are we here? What is the point of it all? Is there really a God? Do you like to travel, take classes, socialize with friends and meet new people? How often do you push yourself beyond your comfort zone?

What does it take to shake up your life? Do you only react and change when pushed by external forces or do you initiate change for personal growth?

Knowing how you and your partner manage change can help you plan an exciting future together or at least give you a glimpse into what living with this person may become.

How often do you read, and what kind of books do you enjoy? Do you exercise, plan parties, join groups, volunteer, or belong to a church?

Do you have a strong desire to keep growing, giving, and learning on this incredible planet? What about your partner?

If you are on the quieter side and unlikely to get involved in your community while your mate is an extrovert who enjoys jumping right into activities, will that create friction? Can you find an acceptable balance?

Cheryl and Mike are an example of an acceptable balance that didn't start out that way. Mike loved talking to strangers. He would start a conversation at the bus stop, in a restaurant or at the grocery checkout. Cheryl found this odd. She asked him, "Do you know that person?" Mike replied, "No, but what an interesting person." Cheryl resented Mike's outgoing demeanor. When Mike started talking, engaging strangers, Cheryl said she found it annoying. Mike said he found it strange that Cheryl would pass someone on the street and not say good morning unless she knew them. Eventually, Cheryl realized that Mike's behavior pushed her further into her own reserved personality. Over time, Mike became more sensitive to Cheryl's reserved nature. Meanwhile, Cheryl began to relax a little and enjoyed participating in the conversations Mike started.

It is obvious that a couple doesn't have to share all interests.

Many couples I talked with had diverse interests. They accepted and enjoyed those differences in each other. Francis and Bill are an example of enjoying the differences.

Francis has a full time job with little free time during the day. Bill is semi-retired with lots of leisure time to hike, bike, golf and visit friends. Francis said she felt as though she was letting Bill down because of her full work schedule. Bill enjoyed seeing her in the evenings and weekends. He has a circle of friends to spend time with during the week while Francis is busy with work. He assured Francis that he understood her work enjoyment and commitment. He found the time apart strengthened his desire to see her when they did have together time.

Knowing your partner's level of curiosity will help evaluate your areas of compatibility. This can provide an opportunity to engage in activities you may never have considered prior to meeting them.

Are you a curious George/Georgette?

_____

_____

_____

Is your partner a curious George/Georgette?

_____

_____

_____

Circle your compatibility score   1   3   5

Question 25

Communication

What was your role in the demise of your last relationship?

Have you ever known someone who points to everyone else's failings for the disappointments in their life? Be cautious of those who claim to be a victim and always blame the other person for the failure of their relationships.

When I hear someone badmouthing their former mate and listing only the ugliness they experienced with them, I have to stop and wonder if they have taken time to reflect on their role in the demise of the relationship. It's easy to create a story in our heads and tell it so often that it becomes our truth: It's my story and I'm sticking to it. This leaves little room for other possible explanations as to why the relationship failed, and worse, does not allow an opportunity to discover the lessons learned from the relationship.

Another way of discovering your partner's role in the past is to ask, "What did you learn from your last relationship?" If they launch into a tirade of what a jerk that person was, then they may have missed the point or they are still too emotionally hurt to review it more objectively.

Janice shared with me that she had been alone for a few years and had a fantasy of the bad boy type when she met Joel at a dance. He lit up her fantasy and before she stopped to catch her breath and look beyond his tough guy appearance and smooth lines, they were hot and heavy and off into trance land. It was only after a month of passion and play that she realized she was making all the effort and he was happy to accommodate her sexual appetite but not much more.

She awoke from this fantasy hurt, exhausted, and angry with him. After taking some time to lick her self-inflicted wounds, she realized she was the one who chased the fantasy and got exactly what she desired. Joel was simply a player in her dream and doing a fine job of portraying the bad boy.

Ross met a woman online and through a few exchanges thought they had some common interests. They met, hit it off, and began a fun and passionate chapter together. After two months, he realized she was not very honest with him. He had "fallen in trance (love)," but he realized she did not line up with most of his pillars of compatibility. Yes the sexual chemistry was fine, but he discovered she had plans with other men. He realized a long-term monogamous partnership would not have worked with her. Ross admitted, "Although the break-up was painful at first, I am grateful for what I learned." She was a knowledgeable nutritionist, and he gained some helpful diet tips.

Ross is quick to say, "I always wonder why this person came into my life and what we needed to share." The expression, "Some for a reason, some for a season and some for a lifetime," may provide insight when we are ending a relationship.

Hopefully, each of us learns from our past relationships and becomes better equipped to recognize what we want in our next one. It is comforting to surround yourself with family and friends after a break-up. With emotional pain comes a healing time. Do not be fooled into thinking you are the saint and your ex is the sinner. It takes two to tangle and sometimes we get caught up in everyone's words of support and justification regarding what kind of jerk you just left. This leaves little room for growth and discovery about our own behavior. Of course any abusive behavior is a clear signal to end a relationship.

Sometimes, a real friend will help you review the relationship from both points of view and not just be your wingman or *yes* friend.

Relationships require effort. They take on-going negotiation, compromise, and attention. With continued effort, honesty, patience and time, we can grow them into loving, joyful, and supportive unions. They also provide valuable insights into our own psyche and roles we play in their success or demise.

What was your role in the demise of past relationships?

_____

_____

_____

What was your partner's role in the demise of past relationships?

_____

_____

_____

Circle your compatibility score   1   3   5

Question 26

Communication

How do you handle stress or conflict?

"Do you flee, fight or faint?"

In the early part of a new relationship, we are generally on our best behavior, keep our worries and stresses close to our chest and do not necessarily reveal our coping methods. Do you know how you deal with stress? How does your partner handle stress?

How easy is it for you to express your wants, concerns, and disappointments? Do you present yourself with smiles and exuberance, even though there are issues between you that leave you feeling sad, scared, or depressed?

Do you strike out with verbal or physical aggression, or do you become silent and withdrawn when things are not going your way? Are you afraid to express your thoughts and feelings?

Mark tells me he grew up in a home of suppressors. Open discussion, anger, excitement or arguments were discouraged at the first sign of raised voices. He admits he still finds it hard to raise his voice and face confrontation.

Marlene grew up with five siblings in a very loud home. As she describes it, "You learned early to yell and be aggressive if you wanted to be heard or get your fair share." She has an instinctive response when faced with disagreement to get louder and more intense with her partners. Imagine her dating someone like Mark.

How do you handle other people's points of view when they are different from yours?

Can you manage a healthy conversation with someone who does not share your opinions? Are you able to put yourself in their shoes and appreciate their point of view, or do others have to see the world the way you do?

Patsy admits, "I need a few drinks before I can relax and begin to share my feelings or be open to intimacy." Hans found this challenging, and shared he liked to address issues straight on and in the moment.

Do you run from disagreement or confrontation? Do you have difficulty dealing with stress? Do you disassociate from conflict? Do you swallow or suppress your feelings with silence, alcohol, or keeping busy? Some people have found healthy ways to release their stress by working out or talking things out. Others choose to seek counsel from those they trust.

Newly married, Susan shared that she was conversing with her husband one night, and it got a little heated. He raised his hand and she flinched. He asked, "What just happened?" She confessed she thought he was going to hit her. He was shocked and asked where the heck did that reaction come from? She explained that in her past, men had struck her when they had a disagreement. He assured her he would never assault her. She had some work to do on trusting him and he learned not to make any sudden moves during an argument.

Learning to stand your ground and voice your thoughts, even if they are contrary to your partner's, may take time and effort. If you are with someone who does not allow you to express your opinions without ridicule or aggression, you may want to rethink your reason for wanting to share a life with them.

Curtis dated Kit for three months and began to fall in love, but he recognized some issues that needed discussion. He told me each time he attempted to voice his concerns and ask for some discussion Kit became very defensive and said, "If that's how you feel, I guess we're done. What is there to talk about?"

He was dumbfounded, since he really wanted to create a future with her and was extending himself so they could have a conversation about his concerns and hopefully build a platform of communication for future issues. He remained calm but disappointed by her reaction.

He set his concern aside for the time being and continued enjoying their time together. A month later while he was travelling, she ended the relationship with an e-mail. He was completely surprised and deeply saddened. In retrospect, he understood her strategy. She had shared that in her past there had been physical abuse and dishonesty from previous mates. Whenever she felt scared, or at the first sign of disagreement, she would leave to avoid the possible pain that might happen. Curtis was unfamiliar with this type of behavior and since the door was closed to resolving their issues, he was left to move on.

Michael met Bev at a friend's wedding and they immediately hit it off. He was a student and finishing a degree at university on the east coast of the United States. Bev lived on the west side of the country. They visited each other and began a passionate relationship. Michael was committed to finishing his degree and finding work in his field. After two months, Bev invited him to move to her city and live with her. He was flattered, but remained focused on completing his studies. He had invested years in his education and was happy to continue seeing her. She became insistent on his moving in with her or she would break it off. He was taken aback by this demand. She wanted it her way and she broke it off. He was saddened by this action, but recognized some important signs of how she dealt with her own needs. A month later she called pleading to reunite and apologizing for her earlier demands. He was not interested and glad he got a preview of her impulsive needs. Her way of dealing with stress was not one he welcomed.

Dianne had a busy life as a paralegal. Michael worked from a home office. Sometimes,

after a stressful day, Dianne would come home and begin criticizing the house and find fault with little things that were not kind to Michael. He quickly recognized a pattern and asked her what happened in the office that upset her. In time, she realized this was her way of releasing her stress, although directed at the wrong person. Through some discussion she decided on days like these it was best for her to go for a long walk before coming home so she could defuse her tension and not dump it on her partner.

Some couples establish guidelines for discussing difficult issues and they work hard to abide by them so their conversations do not get out of hand and escalate into personal attacks or running away.

It's best to recognize that some individuals need more time and space before making a decision. Insisting that someone gives you an answer immediately when you demand it is not always productive.

Mitch was struggling with some job duties and had some unforeseen financial issues come up. His girlfriend Fran wanted to take a winter holiday with him. He was a little unsure if he could get away or afford a vacation. Fran was very much in need of some time away in the sun and so she really pushed for an answer. He tried to explain that he needed a few weeks to get things sorted out, but she was insistent on going on a holiday. This caused some tension between them and she eventually just booked a holiday with a girlfriend. He was disappointment, but confessed to me that he learned quite a bit about her decision making process.

The saying, "Force negates," may push people away from you. Accepting that each person has a unique timeline for response, especially on issues that are sensitive or scary for them, will create a safe place for dialogue, reflection, and resolution.

If there are stresses or conflicts that you cannot resolve with your lover, then seeking professional help may prove some answers. If this does not bring some progress or a healthy outcome, you may want to re-consider if this is the place you want to live.

How do you handle stress and conflict?

_____

_____

_____

How does your partner handle stress and conflict?

_____

_____

_____

Circle your compatibility score   1   3   5

Question 27

Communication

Are you more comfortable talking to your friends and family than your partner?

Do you find it easier to talk about the issues that concern you with someone other than your new partner? Feeling comfortable to share your concerns with this new person will serve you now and for years to come. If you can't have an open dialogue with your lover, how will they know when either of you is fostering unhealthy or unexpressed feelings?

Thomas dated someone for almost two years before he discovered how much gossip and conversation she shared with friends about their personal experiences. He felt betrayed that she did not honor the intimacy of their life together. He thought this behavior sabotaged their relationship.

Sometimes you may just have to bounce your thoughts off of old friends or family before you are ready to share them with your lover. Hopefully, in time you will find ways to speak with your partner first on important matters between you. You may use the five pillars of compatibility to explore what areas need discussion with your partner.

You may be used to sharing the details of your day with family and friends and it has not dawned on you that some things within your relationship should remain private. Some men I spoke to share that they do not want to hear all the details of their partner's day and were alright with their partner sharing that conversation with others. Guidelines that determine what is shared with family and friends and what remains private will ensure a strong, trusting relationship.

If there are aspects of your new relationship that you are uncomfortable talking about with your lover, that may be a red flag of deeper issues between you. Navigating this new territory may take some time and practice.

Are you more comfortable talking to your friends and family than to your partner?

_____

_____

_____

Is your partner more comfortable talking to their friends and family than to you?

_____

_____

_____

Circle your compatibility score   1   3   5

Question 28

Communication

What was your childhood and family life like?

"Lie down on my couch, please."

This is one of the most important questions of the entire checklist. Our childhood experiences establish the foundation for all future relationships. Some believe that our personality is permanently determined in the first seven years of our lives.

Neglected children who did not receive proper nutrition, affection, and encouragement have a much harder time connecting to others.

Knowing about your partner's childhood may foreshadow potential issues in your future together.

I have met both men and women who were treated like princes/ses their entire lives and never really had to work or plan for most of the things they have. Their parents, in most instances, came from humble beginnings and worked hard to create a better life for their children. Not wanting them to experience their earlier hardships, they went overboard and spoiled them. The parents learned that hard work produced beneficial results but their children missed this lesson. As everything was planned and handed to them, they failed to appreciate the things they had received without effort. This created a mind set of expectation and entitlement.

Domenic shared how it was valuable for him to learn about his new girlfriend Mindy's childhood, because it was so different from his. To date a woman who had such high lifestyle demands left him feeling inferior and stressed. He admitted he did not want to replace her father's role of provider. He confessed he wanted a partner who was willing to work equally hard to create the life they both wanted.

Doug dated a woman that never knew her birth father. Nancy shared that it was only as an adult she sought out her biological Dad and was able to spend a little time with him before he died. She told Doug about the mental and physical abuse she endured from her single mother and older brother, and how she ran away at sixteen and lived on the street before going into foster care. Doug found this hard to hear at first, but realized it was very valuable information in learning about her behavior. Knowing that she had lived in a world where people abandoned her from a young age helped him understand her trust triggers. Whenever Nancy stayed at his home, she never unpacked her bag, but always kept it ready in case she needed to make a quick exit. Doug found this odd. The differences in their upbringings were one of the key factors that led to the relationship's eventual demise.

Were you an only child and does your new love come from a big family? How will this affect your interaction and desire for a family? Are you close with your parents, siblings and relatives, or only visit on holidays? This may in turn cause some problems when social or family events come up. Do you come from an alcoholic family? Do you have a drinking problem? Contrary to what some believe, the experiences of our youth tag along with us in adulthood and into our intimate relationships. We need to keep our eyes wide open and decide early if we want to be with someone whose earlier life and traumas still affect their behavior and relations with us. Some believe the apple does not fall far from the tree, and others have made a conscious choice to improve and become a different person than the one from their childhood.

Cheryl, an only child, was raised in a loving and supportive family. Her parents continue to be a big part of her life. After a serious accident, it was recommended that she seek counseling to help her cope with the psychological effects of being sidelined for a few months. The therapist wanted to delve into her childhood issues, but she was quite happy with her childhood and had nothing strange, painful or resentful to discuss. "It was almost as if he was trying to get me to make stuff up," she told me.

Not everyone has demons in their closet that affect their adult behavior and relationships. Of course we all have disappointments, losses and some pain from our childhood, but these experiences helped us to learn and mature.

It is helpful to know of any mental illness in someone's past and present. Learning about depression, bi-polar or other conditions may change how far you want to travel with this new person or how you can be supportive as you grow together.

Carol grew up in a housing project with three siblings and a tough European father who rarely expressed any emotion or affection. She leaned on her mother for the attention she needed as a child. Barry grew up a few blocks away in the same neighborhood. He had two loving parents, though his mother was quite reserved and introverted. He also had three siblings. Carol and Barry crossed paths as young teens, but did not see each other again until they met at the wedding of a mutual friend three decades later. They began a relationship and at first shared a lot in common due to their similar childhood upbringing. The first few months were filled with fun and recognition of mutual life experiences. Then as with most relationships, the real issues began to arise.

Neither of them liked their careers. Carol had been through a tough divorce and had a strained relationship with her children. She also had a drinking problem. Carol pushed for a stronger commitment and wanted to marry Barry. He had never married and feared making a commitment because he had disturbing memories of growing up in a family that rarely had enough and he did not want to find himself living the life of his father. He treasured his freedom and did not want to be with Carol every day. Neither of them was willing to make the effort to deal with their issues and so they came to an impasse and separated.

Our childhood does not have to match that of our lovers, but if we have similar emotional experiences as children it may increase the odds of compatibility.

Growing up with similar values, cultural and religious backgrounds often makes it easier to connect with another person, but there are many examples of people from different social, cultural, and religious backgrounds that have fallen in love and found common ground to create a life together.

Take time to reflect on your histories, how they complement each other and what challenges you may face.

What was your childhood and family life like?

_____

_____

_____

What was your partner's childhood and family life like?

_____

_____

_____

Circle your compatibility score   1   3   5

Question 29

Communication

Do you have regrets?

"I could have, should have, would have…"

Having made choices that you regret, wish you could change and are not proud of is normal. However, dwelling on past experiences with anger or sadness can affect how you embrace life today.

Some use alcohol, food, or other distractions to mask or avoid pain from past decisions that they cannot reconcile. Knowing about your partner's regrets may provide insight into their willingness to take risks, be open, and plan your future together.

Their attitudes about money, sex, communication, caring and commitment may be heavily swayed by a past they cannot let go of. Hopefully, you have met someone who draws on their history and is inspired to create a promising future with you.

Rick was a compulsive complainer and spent much of his time criticizing his world and focusing on his problems instead of the blessings in his life. He met Sheila and it didn't take her long to recognize his strong inner critic that punished and distorted his view on things. She told me it was easy to see that they wouldn't travel the same path together. She ended their relationship after only three dates.

I have tried to reframe situations with friends when they get stuck on this road of complaining and focusing on all the reasons they cannot move forward. I call it being a prisoner in the "valley of excuses." Offering another point of view can sometimes shift their attention to a more positive perception. However, if they are committed to only voicing their disappointments with their life, this will eventually wear on you.

I was fortunate to have found a love match through the process of writing this book. I continue to be inspired by my wife's optimism and happy spirit as we create a life together.

We have all made choices we may not be proud of or would do differently if given another chance. Accepting our decisions and learning from them allows us to move forward.

Asking someone you care about if they have regrets and what they have learned from their past choices will reveal some important insights for you both.

Do you have any regrets?

_____

_____

_____

Does your partner have any regrets?

_____

_____

_____

Circle your compatibility score   1   3   5

Question 30

Communication

How is your health?

I asked a server in a fancy restaurant while writing this book, "How do you know when you are in love?" She replied, "Until we have faced some serious challenge together, I would not know if I was in love with anyone."

The state of someone's health could be such a challenge for you. Learning about their lifestyle and family history of illness will help you determine how much time and energy you want to invest with them.

Dating someone who is a heavy smoker, drinker, or drug user may affect both your present relationship and your future together. If someone has an illness or condition that needs on-going treatment and care, you will have to consider the quality of your time together and the length of the relationship. That may not be an issue at all for someone you truly love, but knowing about someone's physical and mental health is important for you in deciding what kind of commitment you are willing to make.

Daniel contracted herpes from a casual encounter in his early twenties, and now at thirty-one finds it hard to find a girlfriend to be intimate with. He uses protection during sex, but his medical condition has scared off a number of women.

Congresswoman Gabrielle Gifford from Arizona was shot in the head in 2011 and almost died. Her husband, Mark Kelly, showered her with unwavering love and support. He exemplifies the commitment he made when they wed, "in sickness and health." She continues to make tremendous progress with his love and support. Did he know her state of health would take a dramatic turn on that sunny morning in Tucson? Of course not, but he knew whom he fell in love with and what he needed to do to sustain their marriage and navigate through this turbulent chapter in their lives.

Gail and Michael had been married for fifteen years, when Michael was diagnosed with multiple sclerosis. Gail knew his health would eventually decline and she would have to play a much greater role as his caregiver. She also knew it would limit their choices together. They made a commitment to practice a healthy lifestyle and this delayed the onset of his debilitating symptoms. She loved him plain and simple and would stand beside him as he met the new challenges of this illness.

Robert and Patricia started dating and really enjoyed each other's company. She had severe allergies and constantly complained about what they ate, where they ate, an environment they visited, or some other ache or pain. He was not sure how much was real or imagined, but her complaining began to take its toll on his desire to be with her. In time, Robert was honest to share that he realized he could not cope with all these health-related problems she claimed to have, and he moved on.

Do you know the history of your partner's mental health or their family legacy of emotional or mental illness? This is an important factor to consider when making a commitment to them.

Do they take a lot of medication and for what? These are reasonable questions if you plan on living with or marrying them.

It may be too early in the relationship to know what people are made of when the going gets tough, but keep your eyes open for the qualities your partner demonstrates when challenges present themselves to you.

How is your health?

_____

_____

_____

How is your partner's health?

_____

_____

_____

Circle your compatibility score   1   3   5

Question 31

Communication

What is your biggest fear?

There are so many fears that can pre-occupy us that we never get started on our goals. Life can be tough and sometimes we have to fall numerous times before we wake up, stand up and take action in a new direction. Once we learn the lessons we can make better choices. This includes finding the right love match.

It is easy to compromise and create a life with someone to hide out with and avoid your true passions and desires. Hopefully, you will find someone who will cheer you on, hold your hand and remind you often to "go for it." Having a mate who criticizes, dissuades, and holds you back can be a death sentence.

Fear makes us behave strangely and can cloud our memory of our uniqueness. If your lover is not your biggest supporter, confidante, and trusted source of encouragement, why are you with them?

Are you a victim of your own irrational fears of being alone or inadequate? Have you dropped your values, standards and needs to avoid being single? Have you given up on finding a love match?

In my book, Fearless Living, I identified four primary roots of fear.

1. **Lack of knowledge**. If we have not taken the time to learn about ourselves, others, the world we want to create, and the necessary steps needed to achieve our dreams, then this lack of awareness can keep us stuck in fear and continuing to make poor choices in partners.

2. **Lack of experience**. I often say to young people that they should date a few people before they jump into a serious relationship or marriage. The more experience we have with different people the more we learn about what we want and what we don't want in a mate. Believing one person can be everything to us is both naïve and dangerous.

3. **Real danger**. Yes there are real threats in this life and knowing what is risky or dangerous and heeding that inner voice that says stop, run and change course can sometimes save us a lot of heartache and possibly our life. Happily, this type of fear rarely confronts us. If you find yourself with someone who treats you disrespectfully or abusively, run now.

4. **Lack of faith**. The antidote to fear is faith. When fear has us believing there is no hope, answer or happiness, we need to have faith. The greater your faith in yourself or others, the lesser your fear. Faith can come from past experiences where you overcame obstacles, a spiritual belief, leaning on others who support you, but most of all from yourself. By remembering your gifts, abilities, and past successes, you can persevere and create the life and the love you desire.

The good news is that most fears are all between our ears and do not ever happen.

Susan Jeffers, in her book, *Feel the Fear and Do It Anyway*, says, "80% of what we worry about never happens." I agree.

We can choose what to remember about our life experiences. We can tell ourselves the same outdated stories that only reinforce our fears and continue to limit our adventures, or we can update the story, choose to focus on all that is working in our lives and go for it.

Our greatest gift is the ability to change and choose a different kind of person as a partner from those who did not nourish, encourage, or truly love us. Chalk the past up to a learning stage and embrace your future with a clear vision of what you desire and deserve.

What are your biggest fears?

_____

_____

_____

What is your partner's biggest fear?

_____

_____

_____

Circle your compatibility score   1   3   5

Communication compatibility Rating Review

You have now completed all the questions on the Compatibility pillar — Communication

Total the number of #1s = little in common, #3s = some things in common and #5s = very compatible

1 ___ 3 ___ 5 ___

You have now reviewed 31 questions. Congratulations.

Pillar Four: Caring

Question 32

Caring

Does your partner show interest in your life?

There is a country music song that explores a relationship where the woman only talks about her life. The singer responds, "Let's talk about me." Have you ever found yourself in a similar relationship?

How often do you demonstrate interest in your new love's life? Do you ask about their day, work, hobbies, passions, and family? Are you learning more about them and spending more time in their world, than they do in yours, or is there a balance? Someone who only talks about themselves and how busy and important their life is, is waving a big warning flag alerting you they might be the most important person in the room.

Denise met Chuck on a first date in a café. He asked her one question about herself and then proceeded to talk about himself for thirty minutes without a pause. Denise was grateful for having this experience so early and realizing this was not the man she wanted for a love match.

I have known Cee for over a decade. In all this time she has never asked me once about my work, my life, or my family. I find this odd, but realize we have a pleasant friendship; we enjoy each other's company; we have great conversations and I accept that she prefers to stay in the moment. Through this friendship, I have learned that I could never be involved with someone like her on a more intimate level, but she is kind, generous and very interesting to converse with.

Do you want to play second fiddle with someone who believes his or her life is more interesting or important than yours? Does this new person always find themself in some drama consuming all the air in the room with the events of their day? Are you relegated to a supporting role as their enabler, cheerleader and therapist?

Occasionally, we face overwhelming challenges and need emotional support from an intimate partner, but if this happens regularly, you may question why you are cast repeatedly in this supporting role. However, if you like being the caretaker and enabler and you thrive on the drama, then you may have found a perfect match for your needs.

Pete dated an attractive woman who appeared to be very interested in his world. When he told her he was a poet, she asked to read his latest work. He gave her a copy of his new book. A few days later, he called to say hi. She said she was going to stay home that night to read his book. He was encouraged by her comment, but never heard from her again. I guess she didn't like his book. It may take time to determine if someone is genuine or just playing a role. Pete admitted to me that he had been easily side-tracked by the initial sexual attraction with this woman, but was glad it did not continue.

Soon after, he began an online chat with another woman who was very interested in his work. She found a copy of his book, called him and expressed her excitement about reading his work. Pete was touched by this gesture. They had some nice conversations about his writing, which led to a natural progression into other common interests they shared. They continue to date and enjoy each other's lives.

Stay awake to the amount of time a potential mate spends talking about themselves and how often they show sincere interest in your world.

Does your partner show interest in your life?

_____

_____

_____

Do you show interest in your partner's life?

_____

_____

_____

Circle your compatibility score   1   3   5

Question 33

Caring

Are you trying to change me?

There is a saying, "A woman marries a man expecting he will change, but he doesn't, and a man marries a woman expecting that she won't change, but she does."

If your partner is a healthy, secure, intelligent and a capable person, then why would they need to change, control, or direct your behavior? Accepting another is not always easy. If you have an expectation of what you want someone else to be to make you feel better or more secure about yourself, you are heading down an alley marked trouble.

"Oh, he will quit smoking once we get serious," and "I can help him stop drinking so much," stated Claire, as she talked to me about her last boyfriend. She admitted she invested a lot of time and energy trying to change him without any results.

If someone is a slob, has addictions, or is just different from you and the way you prefer things, you have a choice to make. You can focus on what you like about them and accept the differences, or move on. Unfortunately, it's not always that clear of a choice for most of the people I interviewed for this book. Some want to wear the badge of enabler, caretaker, doormat or controller. They admitted in hindsight that trying to change anyone without an invitation was futile. However, if your lover asks for your support and ideas, it may work wonderfully for you both.

Greg lived with an alcoholic and after six months concluded she was more in love with her bottle than him. He realized he could not change her, and expressed what he wanted in his life. He told her, "I want a partner who places me first in their life." He wished her well and left. This was not an easy choice he told me, but he recognized his care and support were not enough for his girlfriend to change her behavior and choices.

I found it takes courage to honestly admit what we can accept in someone and what is too tall an order. I like the expression, "The older we get, the more we become more of who we are." The challenge is realizing if you can accept someone as they are for your love match.

Elizabeth shared, that she was told her entire life, "It would be her partner who brought her happiness and fulfillment." She had huge expectations that once she found the "right" someone to marry, only then she would be complete. This belief placed a huge pressure on both her partner and her unrealistic expectations of what marriage was supposed to be. It was only after an ugly divorce and dating numerous men that she came to understand her happiness was dependent on herself. This realization was a major relief for her.

Dorothy lived on a street where some of her neighbors hung their clothes outside to dry. She thought this was an eyesore and each time she looked out her kitchen window she would comment on the nerve of her neighbor Sally hanging her dirty clothes for all to see. She told me she would complain to her husband about the lack of respect for others in her community. One day she looked outside and noticed something was different. She commented to her husband, "Well, it's about time, she must have changed detergents. At least those clothes look cleaner." He replied, "Yes, and I guess washing our windows helped."

Marjory was an elder in her church, and very respected by many people who imagined what her personal life was like and tried to emulate it. At a workshop she led in church one day, she shared that her husband, of thirty odd years, was not a member of their church and enjoyed playing poker, smoking, and drinking with his buddies once a month. Admirers were shocked. How she could remain with someone like that? They were looking at Marjory's marriage through "their window" and began to realize how judgmental they were. Some came to apologize and said, "We had no right to judge or change you."

I have certainly been guilty of spouting my unsolicited beliefs on others only to find myself in a conflict. I have been the recipient of such uninvited advice and it made me uncomfortable. The idea that "force negates," has been true for me whether in business, social or romantic relationships. Unless I am asked for my opinion, or it is life threatening, I am learning to remain quiet when someone acts in a way that does not match mine.

Acceptance is the key to success in any relationship and one of the hardest attributes to practice, because we all have an ego that believes we know best. We each have agendas that we want others to accept and often do not see the person for who they really are. We convince ourselves in time and with some effort they will change their ways, preferably to ours.

Are you trying to change me?

_____

_____

_____

Am I trying to change you?

_____

_____

_____

Circle your compatibility score   1   3   5

Question 34

Caring

How is your partner caring and generous?

Do you consider yourself a generous person? Do you like giving to others, whether in big or in small ways? How often to you pick up an extra cup of coffee or your partner's favorite ice cream? Have you ever stopped into a store because you saw something in the window you knew your partner would like? How often do you plan and pay for an activity as a sign of your appreciation for your partner? Do you limit your generosity to buying gifts only after receiving a gift first, or only on official occasions like a birthday, an anniversary, or Christmas?

I like to surprise my wife with flowers, chocolates, or a card to remind her of my feelings for her. Likewise, I appreciate similar gestures when she invites me out to lunch, purchases a book I would enjoy, or takes time to select lingerie. Simple gestures such as a text, e-mail or phone call just to say, "Hi, I was thinking of you with a smile on my face," are also appreciated.

Dan fell in love with a woman who showered him with kind, loving and very appreciative messages in the first few weeks of their relationship. Toni wore sexy outfits a few times, left him love notes, but slowly in the second month this behavior stopped. Dan realized he was the one doing most of the calling, paying, loving, planning and expressing. When he gently mentioned it would be nice to get a phone call to hear her voice once in a while, he got a cold, "I don't like talking on the phone." He shared with me that this response snapped him out of his trance and made him realize they were not compatible in this area of communication. He opened his eyes to other differences and he decided not to pursue a long-term commitment.

How often do you compliment your partner? Is it easy for them to say something nice to you? Do they focus on what they like about you and acknowledge it, or do they rarely take the time to compliment, support or demonstrate interest in your appearance, behavior or your being? Worse, are their comments usually about something you have done wrong?

Volunteering is a great indicator of how someone gives back. Do you or your partner contribute to the community? Whenever I hear someone say, "I'm bored. I don't know what to do with my time," I think of volunteering as a way to get out of their own heads and self-indulgence and lend a hand to someone who needs it. Volunteering says a lot about someone else and yourself. This is one more sign of their level of care and compatibility with you.

It helps to acknowledge what level of care you desire. You need to determine what is within your acceptable range of giving and receiving in a relationship. If your norm is to take more than you give, your romance may be short-lived. However, if you find someone who will tolerate your needy nature, you may have found a treasure. If you find you are always giving more that may be become old quickly too. Finding a balance in a love match is ideal.

Taking reality checks periodically can be very insightful. If you are the one giving most of the time and getting little back, then either buy a tee-shirt marked "doormat," ask for what you want, or move on.

How is your partner caring and generous?

_____

_____

_____

How are you caring and generous to your partner?

_____

_____

_____

Circle your compatibility score   1   3   5

Question 35

Caring

How many chefs are in your kitchen?

Do you have to be in control? Does one of you always have to be right? These are warning signals of trouble to come.

I lived with someone who knew everything, forced her opinion on strangers and friends alike, always had an answer, and always had to be in control. It was exhausting.

Who plans most of your activities? Who has higher demands and needs? Who requires more emotional maintenance? These behaviors may be a form of control.

Are you both easy-going and accept the flow as the day unfolds or do you have to have every minute planned? Do you have a need to control your partner or change how they drive, eat, dress, spend or speak? If you believe your way is the right way, you may be in for some turbulent waters ahead.

I like to plan my days with built-in flexibility for surprises and changes. I like a balance between initiating and following someone else's lead. It is too much pressure to always be the one who is calling, planning and making all the effort. It is flattering to have someone else ask me out on a date for a walk, a coffee, or a fun-filled evening.

Moira is a fabulous cook. Bryce, her partner, can barely boil water, but he knows how to fix any appliance, tool or gadget in the house. They realized early what their strengths were and they deferred certain tasks to the other. They have a respectful system of working together and getting things done.

If you must be in control at all times, have a strong need to impose your ideas on your partner, and do not trust this adult to make the right choices for themselves or the two of you, then why do you want a mate? If you need a doormat, go to the department store.

Fern admitted to me, her need to be in charge stems from insecurity. She experienced disappointment from early partners and this convinced her the only one she could rely on was herself. She recognizes her tendency to want to "boss and control" as she puts it, and this she believes helps to avoid the pain of being let down yet again.

The benefits of a good relationship include learning from one another, sharing roles, supporting one another and trusting your partner to handle an issue without interference. Your past relationships do not equal your present one. Trust your partner to shine.

How many chefs are in your kitchen?

_____

_____

_____

Circle your compatibility score   1   3   5

Question 36

Caring

Do your friends and family like this new person?

How do your friends and family feel about this new person in your life? Does your new love fit easily into your social circle? If your friends and family express their feelings, either supportive or cautionary, consider their comments.

Listen to those who have known you a long time and who care about you. If you have concerns about this new person in your life, your family and friends' opinions may provide a needed perspective. Remember, when we fall into trance in the early stages of a relationship, our sensors and willingness to hear others' points of view may be clouded, and comments from those that care about us may be resented or ignored.

Do not consult with individuals who are jealous of you and have their own insecurities or agendas. Talk to people who care about you and have seen your choices in partners. They may provide insight that you cannot see.

If you normally spend a lot of time with family and friends and suddenly you are only spending time with your mate, this could lead to estrangement from those who share your history. If your new lover does not work out, you could end up working hard to regain former friends or risk losing some too.

If you do not have a circle of close friends or strong ties with your family, then your intuition and this list of fifty questions may be a great resource to determine if the person you are dating have the qualities for a long-term love match.

Conversely, do you like their friends and family? If they spend a lot of time socializing with a group of friends, or see their family quite often, it might take some adjusting for you to get to know all of these people. Do you feel comfortable or uncomfortable around them? Have they made an effort to invite you into their circle?

It is normal and healthy to have friends that you socialize with apart from your lover. They may be golf buddies, poker night friends, movie chums or acquaintances you see at a book club. Keep an eye on any attempts by your new love to limit or stop your associations with these people.

Try to be open to listening to objective points of view from family and friends. It may save you emotional and financial difficulty around the corner.

Do your friends and family like this new person?

_____

_____

_____

Do their friends and family like you?

_____

_____

_____

Circle your compatibility score   1   3   5

Question 37

Caring

Where is your "but" scale?

"I like him, but…"

How many "buts" do you include when describing this new person to your family and friends?

"Oh, he is so kind, but he corrects me often. He is so good looking, but he comments on my weight," reports Sarah when describing her new boyfriend.

"She is very smart and funny, but she's always late," confesses Marty after a couple of dates with a new woman.

Do you talk yourself out of listening to your inner voice that knows something is missing in this new person? We can easily ignore the "but" list because of our needs, resistance to be alone, or the belief that this new person will change or we can change them. Small concerns often resolve themselves without mention, but big "buts" or deal breakers should be carefully considered before venturing too far into the romance.

Jennifer was asked out on a date and was afraid. I asked her what she was fearful of, and she replied, "He will be expecting sex." Her history was filled with one-nighters, because she believed the only way men would like her was if she slept with them. She could not believe someone just wanted to get to know her and not just her body.

If someone criticizes your appearance, intelligence, family, or career, think long and hard about continuing to associate with them, even if the sex is great. Tony shared, "It was like being hit by a bus when I met Didi. The sexual pull was irresistible." He admits, "All bets were off and I could not see or hear any of the "buts" standing in front of me. Off I went into trance land." This is a common experience unless we have the resources to stop, take a breath and look at what we really want.

Do you feel less beside this person? If so, that is a huge BUT sign of trouble ahead.

Would you accept this person making the same comments or acting inappropriately to someone you really care about? If not, then why would you settle for such behavior towards yourself?

Everyone has shortcomings you may not relish, but the key is to ensure the yes's outweigh **the buts** in a love match.

Take a moment and review the last few times you spent with this new person and make a list of any obvious "buts" that arise.

Circle your compatibility score   1   3   5

Question 38

Caring

What level is your trust meter on?

On a scale of one to five on a trust meter, five being completely trusting, and one being total lack of trust of this new person, where is your level set right now?

Have you had good experiences with lovers and trust was not an issue, or have you been hurt enough to be skeptical about anyone new in your life? What will it take for you to believe this person is honest, dependable, and open about their life?

If someone needs to know what you do every minute of your day away from them, this may indicate trouble ahead. Learning that your partner was cheated on, lied to, abused, or abandoned, may provide some insight if they are suspicious of you. You may have done nothing wrong to make them distrust you, but their perception may be bias based on their past experience. Hopefully, in time and through new experiences with you, their trust will grow.

Martina stated very clearly to me, "Men are dogs, and I do not trust them. If they cannot get into bed with me they are on to the next one." Obviously, it would take some time to establish any level of trust from a woman like her.

Recognizing the baggage we bring to a new relationship helps us to change our behavior towards this new person. If we project our past onto them, we should not be surprised to have the same issues and results surfacing. It takes sincere reflection and honesty to distinguish what is yours, theirs, and our baggage. It's only then that you begin to sort out and drop the past. By taking ownership of our own issues, we can clearly focus on the challenges faced as a new couple. By avoiding this exercise, you risk having your past haunt you and create repeat performances in the present and future.

Helen has been married for 23 years, and she firmly states, "Honesty and trust are the keys to our success."

Control is often an issue with trust. I worked from a home office and every few weeks went into the city to my company's head office. My partner at the time would question me relentlessly on whom I was seeing, where I was staying, and when I would return. It got tiresome and disappointing that she did not trust my honest answers. I later learned she had both cheated and been cheated on, and so her trust meter was unbalanced.

Glen met Dahlia and they went out on a date. He found her attractive, bright and funny.

She was a teacher and he was a speaker and businessman. He shared his past with her and when he asked her what her last name was, she refused to say. He found this odd. He was teaching a course in the next week and invited her to sit in to see what he did for a living and to get to know him a little better. He asked where she taught and again she met with avoidance. When he inquired further about her reluctance to even reveal her surname, she said, "If I tell you my last name, you will check me out on Google." Glen realized she had some issues and was very guarded. He assured her he was simply trying to get to know her. This made no difference and so he chose not pursue this relationship.

If you have lied and deceived your way through past relationships, then pursuing a union with a straightforward, honest and sincere individual may not be the right match for you. If you like game players, bad boys or girls, and are looking for a good time not a long time, tell it like it is upfront and avoid the drama. If you are hooked on emotional, roller-coaster relationships with lots of uncertainty and excitement, then the bad boys or girls might provide exactly what you are accustomed to.

How much does your partner share about the times when you are apart? Geoff dated a woman that he thought he knew and trusted. However, one evening while out to dinner, he asked Annette why she had not returned any of his calls the day before. She replied, "Oh, I was invited to a concert by an old friend and then went to an after party with the band."

He was surprised and disappointed that she did not tell him about the concert or ask if he wanted to go. Geoff was suspicious hearing that she stayed out till 3 a.m. with an old friend whom she had never previously mentioned.

Can you be trusted to spend time alone with friends of the opposite sex? Hopefully, your partner has met your friends and it is not an issue. A partner hiding the fact that they are spending time with friends may be a reason to adjust your trust meter.

As your new relationship evolves, do you trust your partner with your money? Are you comfortable leaving your purse or wallet in the open? Do they hit you up for money, promising to repay you and then conveniently forget to do so?

At some appropriate time, if you choose to live together or discuss marriage, you will need to thoughtfully discuss the management of your banking and expenses.

Could you depend on this new love if you got ill, lost your job or had to move away for work, school or military service?

Can you share intimate details of your health, past, or personal fears and trust they will not criticize you, share this private information or run for the door?

It may be wise to test the level of trust early in the relationship to avoid big surprises down the road. Does your partner flirt with your friends or strangers? Have they given you reason to pause or wonder why they are so interested in your financial affairs, work relationships, family matters, or children?

Frank tried an on-line dating site to meet someone new. He connected with a woman that he had an easy time conversing with on-line. He had never actually spoken to her on the phone or in person, but looked forward to that next stage. After half a dozen exchanges on line, he asked about her family life. She said she had two sons. Innocently, he asked about them just to get an idea of how busy her life was and how this might affect their time together. She gave him a strong reply saying, "My sons are off limits. I don't discuss them with any man." He was surprised by her tone and realized this was a very sensitive issue for her. After some reflection, he realized she might have thought he was searching the site to find single moms with young boys — a perfect source for a pedophile. Yes, there are cheaters, liars and pedophiles in our neighborhoods that can present a kind, friendly and warm persona to earn our trust. Frank understood her protective reply, but concluded he did not want to go any further with her.

Observing how your new love treats your parents, friends and pets may indicate whether or not you can trust them and consider a future together. It takes time before we let down our defenses down.

Staying awake during the initial attraction stage is very important in identifying the signs of mistrust or concern. Disclosure is a gradual process and trust is earned, not assumed.

What level is your trust meter on?

_____

_____

_____

Circle your compatibility score   1   3   5

Question 39

Caring

The Tic-Tock Test

How often are you kept waiting by your partner?

Is your partner on time for dates, appointments and social events? Punctuality is one factor to consider when assessing compatibility. How your lover cares for you, respects your time, and delivers on promises, whether minor or important, is critical to your future together.

Jane was a budding artist who had her hands in many projects to keep her creatively stimulated and to pay her bills. She often over-planned her day, leaving her exhausted and forgetful of appointments with friends. She admitted to me she sometimes found it challenging to find and maintain romantic involvements.

Someone who is chronically late, unorganized and constantly making excuses may be signaling that you are not important enough to make a priority.

Cheryl and Jeff lived together. They fought often about Jeff's lack of punctuality. Cheryl told me she constantly has to remind him of how much time they had before they had to leave. Either he would not be dressed early enough or they would have to return for some forgotten item. Being late for dinners with friends, doctor's appointments or concerts was wearing thin on Cheryl. "It hurt to always be kept waiting," she admits. Regardless of her suggestions to help him with better time management, he did not change his behavior. She wondered, "Is this a man/boy who stills needs a mommy to keep him organized?"

Of course, everyone can be delayed due to work, traffic, and unforeseen events, but someone who cannot keep a commitment with you for a movie date; dinner or other activity is disrespecting you and your time. Some partners have come to accept the tardiness of another and it does not annoy them enough to demand a change. If you can accept this trait in a mate, it may not be an issue.

I believe chronic lateness shows a lack of respect for others. Some may argue it is a time management issue; if so, then some coaching may be helpful. If being kept waiting is a frequent occurrence in your relationship and you are unhappy with it, then brace yourself for continued frustration, disappointment and conflict, or change how you plan events together and allow loads of extra time.

Maureen shared that she has a system with her husband Rick when they have an appointment. They take different vehicles and have agreed if one is going to be late, the other should go ahead and attend whatever it is they planned and the other will catch up. This works for them.

You must decide what your standard of care is and how much time you are willing to invest or lose because of someone else's lateness.

The Tic-Tock Test: How often are you kept waiting for your partner?

_____

_____

_____

Circle your compatibility score   1   3   5

Question 40

Caring

How do you honor your mate?

Aretha Franklin captures the essence of this question in her classic song, *Respect*.

Everyone desires respect. Are you with someone who honors you and values your judgment, talents, and time? Do you look to them for guidance and support at times when you are facing a challenge?

Standing beside someone you respect is a huge asset in building a strong foundation and future with this person.

Kevin lived with Jenna who continually questioned his abilities and choices, and often contradicted or belittled him in front of strangers. This left him feeling inferior and angry. Kevin told me he was chatting with a repairman about a leak in the front of the house when without warning or invitation, Jenna jumped into the conversation, corrected him and took over directing the repairman on how to complete the tasks at hand. Kevin was embarrassed by her forcefulness and need to control. On another occasion, he shares that he went outside to put up a simple sign and again Jenna came charging out of the house and supervised the job correcting his abilities.

There is a kinder and more respectful way for offering your ideas without making someone else feel wrong or inferior. When someone respects us that also leads to trusting our judgment and ability.

Keep your antennas up in the early stages of your involvement because this behavior from your partner may not change. I recall talking to a salesperson in a store and not paying attention to my wife. I was making decisions for us both and not consulting her. She privately told me she felt dismissed by me. This woke me up quickly and I apologized. This was not the way I wanted to honor her and I am glad she spoke up.

Other ways to demonstrate respect for your partner include: being on time for engagements; complimenting their ideas and behavior; supporting their dreams; asking for their input on projects and planning; deferring to them in areas you are not as adept or experienced in; acknowledging their contributions and pointing out to friends and strangers their accomplishments.

The old notion of complimenting someone will give them a swollen head or inflate their ego is outdated. If the people closest to you do not respect and acknowledge you first, it may be a long wait for others too.

How do you honor your mate?

_____

_____

_____

How does your mate honor you?

_____

_____

_____

Circle your compatibility score   1   3   5

Question 41

Caring

"Does your partner like dogs and older folks?"

Do either of you like animals? Does one own a pet? Is either of you allergic to any animal? How will your love or dislike of animals affect living together?

Tom dated Joanne, the owner of a skittish rescue dog. Every attempt made by Tom to be kind to it was rejected. Joanne assured him it was the dog's issue and that he behaved like that with everyone. She did not know the canine's history and so assumed the dog may have been abused or traumatized and was afraid of people. After a few months, Joanne's daughter convinced her mother to rescue a small pony that was going to be put down. One day Tom arrived to find this small horse in the backyard of her urban residential home. Joanne could barely afford to pay her mortgage and now she had added the expense of another animal. Tom was moved by her big heart to help this animal but had some reservations about the financial sense of her decision.

Sara had three dogs and loved to take them for long walks every-day. Jeff, a new man in her life, did not like animals, at least not in his home. Sara loved to volunteer in her community. Jeff had never given his time to any organization other than ones he was paid by. "It was clear pretty earlier on that we had very different attitudes about giving back. Although I was attracted to Jeff physically, his willingness to open up to my pets or community were limited, and I chose to look for a more compatible boyfriend."

Is your partner kind to older folks? Are they sensitive enough to know that older people may need a little more time getting things done or finishing a sentence? If you have older parents or grandparents, are they comfortable interacting with them?

Those who do not like engaging older people should be reminded that one day they will be older and will need someone to talk to and care about them. Besides, there is so much wisdom to garner by befriending mature individuals who have loads of life experiences.

I enjoy hiking every week with a group of senior friends who are old enough to be my parents. Once, Michael, an eighty-year-old asked me, "Why do you hang out with us old farts?" I replied, "I do not see age. I enjoy your spirit and company." It was important to me that my love match shared this perspective with me.

Joan loves cats and dogs and volunteers at the Humane Society walking rescue dogs twice a week. She met Bill at the shelter and they began walking dogs together. She learned a great deal about him during their volunteer time together and eventually asked him out. They have been dating for six months and are now talking about marriage.

Learning about your new love's interest in others, especially animals and older people will reveal a lot to you.

Does your partner like dogs and older folks?

_____

_____

_____

Do you like dogs and older folks?

_____

_____

_____

Circle your compatibility score   1   3   5

Caring compatibility Rating Review

You have now completed all the questions on the Compatibility pillar — Caring

Total the number of #1s = little in common, #2s = some things in common and #3s = very compatible and insert below.

1 ____ 3 ____ 5 ____

You have now reviewed 41 questions. Congratulations.

Pillar Five: Commitment

Question 42

Commitment

Why do you want to get married or not?

This is not a simple question. There are a myriad of reasons to commit to a legally binding agreement with another person. Do you have a fantasy of being married, or have you fallen in love with the image of the wedding day? Have you seriously considered a future with this one person as your life partner? Do your pillars of compatibility line up?

Elizabeth Gilbert, in her book, *Committed*, writes, "The problem with infatuation is that it's a mirage, a trick of the eye and the endocrine system. When you become infatuated with someone, you're not looking at that person; you're just captivated by your own reflection, intoxicated by a dream of completion that you have projected on a virtual stranger."

I have witnessed first-hand four secretaries progress from dating to engagement to the planning of their weddings. In all four cases, it struck me how much time was invested in creating the fantasy of the wedding day and the trappings it entails: the countless hours and arguments about guest lists, florists, videographers, photographers, caterers, banquet halls, and then the honeymoon arrangements. I observed the escalating costs and the many stresses created by this fantasy. Very little time or reflection was given to the person they were committing to and what their lives would be together after the big party.

Are you more willing to invest in a Broadway production type wedding than a lifetime commitment to this person that you claim to love? This can be a tough question to reflect on once you fall into the planning mode of the big day. Please do not get distracted by the festival and forget about the many days and years to follow with this person.

Are you choosing marriage because you do not want to be alone or because you have dated for an arbitrary period? Are you getting pressure from parents or friends that "it is time" for a wedding?

Michael was in a long-term, monogamous relationship with Deborah. After a few years, she began talking about marriage. She shared she did not feel secure just dating, but would feel better if they were married. As she already had two children, that was not the motivation for marriage. Michael told me he was very happy with Deborah and their relationship and had no desire to see anyone else. He loved her and all that they shared together. He tried to tell her security came from within — not from him or a legal contract between them. This was not enough for Deborah and she broke up with him.

A few years later, they communicated again, and Deborah was in a new, four-year relationship but still unmarried. Michael wondered, why she had accepted still being unwed if that was what she believed gave her security.

Are you folding to your family, culture or society's expectation that couples should marry at a certain point in their relationship? We are still early in this new century, but for the first time in many years the number of unmarried couples is equal or slightly ahead of those who have chosen the traditional vows. Marriage is not for everyone and finding a love match does not necessarily include marriage. Two people can love, commit and live together for a lifetime without the need for a formal ceremony.

Scott Peck, the famed author of *The Road Less Travelled*, shared in a talk I attended that he believed there were only two reasons to get married. The first reason was to have a family; historically, children do better with two parents. The second reason was the goal of spiritual development. He knew of no better way to learn about one's self than to share a commitment with another person in the institution of marriage. How many people have you known who had this goal in mind when choosing to marry?

I attended a Catholic wedding and during the marriage ceremony the priest stopped the proceedings, faced the congregation and pointedly asked a number of people, "What is love?" It startled those chosen to respond, but I recognized the importance of his question. He was trying to awaken the couple from their marriage trance to reflect on their words and vows on this special day. Unorthodox maybe, but the point was made, at least on me.

A colleague named Martha admitted to me that her reason for wanting so desperately to get married was not so much the desire to build a life together with another person, but rather, "to have a public event so everyone, including myself, can see that I was finally chosen by another for a life time commitment." She admitted she needed this union to make her feel special. "The big show," as she called the wedding, was the icing she needed on her security cake.

Historically, marriage was an economic arrangement and romantic love was rarely a part of the equation. Many married couples lived on a farm and had children to help grow the crops and share the chores. Working together, they survived in tough times. In some parts of the world, arranged marriages are still the norm and people are thrown together for cultural, economic and religious reasons with passion and love having little to do with the union.

Not everyone wants to get married. I know of some older friends who have been married and divorced. They now date occasionally and have no desire to ever marry again. They realized after the demise of their marriages that they did not want to ever commit to someone on that level again. They are content with their lives, their circle of friends and the freedom of being single.

It is important to know your feelings about marriage before you venture too far with a new person. Refer back to question one: *What kind of relationship are you seeking?* It is a deeper act of commitment to officially wed, and if both parties agree to this next step in the relationship, that is a clear sign of your long-term intentions.

Marriage is also a huge commitment in your financial future? It may add to your standard of living, or conversely, it may reduce your standard of living if you inherit the debts of your spouse. Be cautious if marrying for money is the primary reason for making such an important commitment. If the other pillars are absent from your compatibility picture, it may be a short-lived love match.

If you feel you have found a life mate, someone that understands you and adds to your life on many levels, then marriage might be the natural course for you.

Why do you want to get married or not?

_____

_____

_____

Why does your partner want to get married or not?

_____

_____

_____

Circle your compatibility score   1   3   5

Question 43

Commitment

Describe what a best friend means to you.

Once the initial infatuation, fun and adventure settle down and you begin to face the day to day challenges of work, money, children, family, health, and communication, can you honestly look at this person and recognize them as your best friend or best friend potential?

How do you define a best friend? Your new love may not replace an existing best friend, but they should possess some of the same traits to qualify as a best friend.

Is this someone you trust to share your joys and fears with without concern that they will judge you too harshly or walk away?

As my wife reminds me, "Good friends will help you move, and best friends will help you move a body." When choosing a life mate you want to know they have your back. It may be too early to know how far your partner will go to watch your back, but keeping this in mind will help you stay focused during the getting–to–know-you phase.

Does your lover need to be your best friend? I think they should be one of them.

Although Todd has some female friends who want him to be their best "girlfriend," he frankly admits, "I am not wired that way." He does not have suitable listening or emoting skills, or the interest in every detail of their day. He suggested that they share these needs with a girlfriend. It helps to know what strengths and weaknesses we bring to the relationship.

When the front door of your matrimonial home is closed and you climb into bed at the end of the day, is this the person you can call your closest friend?

Jerry told me he was deeply in love with Lee. While dating, they shared their past and used these experiences to build on their present and future. Jerry learned that Lee had no hesitation in sharing some of their private matters with her girlfriends at work. He felt this was a violation of their bond. He felt strongly that she must stop this practice and he admits, "Her actions made me reconsider how much I was willing to disclose to her in the future." His definition of a best friend includes absolute trust in their confidences.

Have you shared intimate details with your love only to have them thrown back in your face later in an argument, or indiscreetly shared outside the sanctity of your union?

Alice clearly states, "Trust is a main ingredient in defining a best friend." Building trust takes time and many experiences as we learn how much we can rely on and feel secure with our new love.

Relying on your partner to support you emotionally, financially at times, physically if needed, is critical, but equally valuable is trusting them to tell you the truth even when everyone else is avoiding telling you what you may need to hear. A "Yes-man/woman," who will never challenge or disagree with you may not act in your best interests.

Keep in mind; it is unrealistic to expect your mate to be the perfect friend in every situation you encounter. Knowing what you want and expect in a best friend is a good place to start.

Describe what a best friend means to you?

_____

_____

_____

Circle your compatibility score   1   3   5

Question 44

Commitment

How many friends of the opposite sex do you have?

Is your new love comfortable with and accepting of these friends? Some men believe it is not possible to have a friendship with a woman they are not sleeping with. However, I have many female friends whom I love dearly but have no sexual interest in. We are buds who enjoy great conversations and activities together.

If your new love is uncomfortable with your established relationships, you need to discuss what the issues are and decide if you want to continue with someone who is trying to limit or control your time with friends. If they have not dealt with their own trust issues, this may come tumbling down on you. It is normal to reduce the amount of time you spend with your friends once you are in a new relationship, but abandoning the established connections you have can be damaging.

Paula met Richard, and was quickly "falling in love" with him. He had a friend Diane, he had known for many years. He socialized with Diane often and occasionally travelled with her. Paula requested that Richard not see his female friends for a while so they could focus on their new relationship. Richard agreed, but did not realize the impact this decision would have on Diane. He had made plans with Diane to escort her to a graduation ceremony long before he ever met Paula, and then cancelled them on Paula's request. A few months later when the relationship with Paula went sour, Diane had no interest in seeing Richard again. He lost a long-time friend because he was not willing to stand up and tell his new girlfriend that his long-time relationships were not negotiable.

Ideally, you want to share your friends with your new love and broaden your relationship circle.

Jerry was hurt to discover that some "couple" friends he had spent time with while dating a new woman suddenly disappeared when his relationship was over with her. "I found this strange and hurtful since I thought we had a good friendship regardless of whom I was seeing. They simply dropped me off their radar," he confessed to me. Some couples do not know what to do with a single friend.

It is healthy to have a circle of opposite-gender friends. Some men actually find it easier to share their feelings and experiences with women than with other men. I find some men limited in the scope and range of conversation as they are more comfortable in the sports and weather dialogue lane. When I try to share some deeper thoughts or feelings, they seem unwilling or uninterested.

When we have friends of the opposite sex, we can connect better with our partner. Spending time with opposite-gender friends without any sexual agenda can add to our awareness and comfort level with our lover.

One of my dearest friends, Charlotte, whom I have known for many years, married and moved to another state. We had always kept in touch and I was invited to her twentieth wedding anniversary celebration. Her husband Bill was quite suspicious of me, and had conjured up some story that I was a former boyfriend and could not fathom that we could be just good friends. Charlotte and I had met at a class years earlier and maintained our friendship. I found it amusing that Bill was so concerned about my visit. Once I arrived, we sat and chatted alone and he realized I was not a threat and that he had overreacted. We got along fine from that point on.

Jeff was married to Gloria for seventeen years and they had three children. After some turbulent times, they decided to separate. Rather than a costly divorce, they settled on a financial arrangement. They chose to put their children above their disagreements and maintained a friendly relationship. They each began new romantic lives. Jeff met Patty and they decided to live together. Gloria was aware of their relationship and was happy for Jeff. In time, they all became friends and occasionally shared family events. Having three children was a fact they had to address. They accepted that there would be times when everyone would be together and so they decided to take the high road and in time their friendship grew.

Terry was dating Rochelle. She introduced him to her biking friend, Peter. One night a group of friends rented a movie and Terry was invited to share the evening. Rochelle sat on the couch, snuggled up to Peter and left Terry sitting alone. Terry felt rejected and wondered what the real relationship was between Rochelle and Peter. He confronted Rochelle later and asked her if there was a romantic history between her and Peter. Rochelle assured him there was none. Terry requested that she refrain from displays of affection with other men because it made him uncomfortable. A greeting hug was fine, but snuggling up on the coach was not okay with him.

Being truthful with your new love about the history and extent of your relationships with friends of the opposite gender is critical in avoiding trust and boundary issues. By respecting your partner's feelings and behaving appropriately with friends of the opposite sex, you will avoid potential and unnecessary arguments.

How many friends of the opposite sex do you have?

_____

_____

_____

How many friends of the opposite sex does your mate have?

_____

_____

_____

Circle your compatibility score: 1   3   5

Question 45

Commitment

Tell me about your past relationships?

"Do you really want to open this door?"

Learning about your lover's past romances builds on the last question. Best friends generally know about their partner's past. It is natural to be curious about your partner's history, but consider carefully your timing and need for details.

Fantasizing that you are the first and only love of this person's life (unless you are a teenager) is unrealistic and childish. Imagining your lover's romantic history without knowing the truth can cause unnecessary stress and lead to unfounded insecurity.

Age is an important factor in learning about the past. If you are older and dating someone who has been married once or maybe more, you may broach your respective histories differently than if you are young, new to dating and this is one of your first serious relationships.

Hopefully, your past relationships have helped you both learn and grow, and become a better match for each other. As we get older, we become more comfortable with the decisions that have shaped us, including our choices in past partners.

Sid, a man in his sixties, had been a widower for about two years when he was introduced to Lisa, a recent widow of nine months. Neither of them had any interest in marrying again or even dating so soon after their losses. Some friends had suggested they might just want a new friend to socialize with. They agreed to e-mail and found they had many common interests and life experiences. Since they were not contemplating dating, they were more open about past experiences. Finally, they started chatting on the phone and as Lisa said, "The first time I heard his voice, I knew this was more than just a new friend." They quickly began to feel love for one and other. They found many matches in their pillars of compatibility, and within six months they were married. They both enjoy a new life together and as Lisa says, "It was as if our ex-spouses had planned for us to get together so we would not be alone."

Some specific knowledge of your new love's past is important if you are thinking of furthering the relationship with them. These *Love Match* questions will come in handy during this process.

Edith and Harry were friends for many years. They had dated with their spouses many times and had a great history together. When both of their respective partners died, they leaned on each other for support and care during their losses. In time, they became a couple and in their early eighties decided to marry. This is one of my favorite examples of knowing about someone's past and letting it provide comfort and love.

Do they have any health issues that were a result of unprotected sex? This could greatly affect your willingness to make love with them. Ignorance could be fatal!

Were they abused? This may play a critical role in how they interact and trust you.

Do they share their thoughts and feelings openly with you, or are they guarded and secretive?

Have they always depended on their spouse for their financial security or are they independent? If your lover has had financial difficulties, cannot hold a job, and bounces from one project to another without completion, this may have significance for you. Conversely, if you meet someone who shares your dreams and commitment to them, you may have found a partner to help achieve them.

Becoming intimate with a new person may be very natural and mutual, or it may require patience if one of you is more willing and the other needs more time.

Some partners prefer not to know about the number of lovers you have had because they can accept you for who you are today. Others may be very welcoming of your past and how it has shaped you to where you are in the present.

In some cultures, having had past lovers or being divorced may label you in an unkind and unfavorable way.

Dave met a very vivacious woman who just knocked him off his feet. She was energetic, adventurous, and loved being outdoors. They laughed and conversed on a variety of subjects. He opened his heart and thought he had found a true love match.

In time, he learned she had many previous lovers and this shook his confidence. He started thinking he was just another guy along her road. He retreated in thinking about a future with her. She would casually mention her previous three husbands and again this affected his interest in pursuing her. His trust began to wane whenever they were apart. It was not long after that he realized he could not accept her past and he broke it off. Within a few weeks, he learned she had already found someone new.

Sometimes, sharing too much too fast can jeopardize a new relationship. There is a suitable time and place to learn about your partner's past with the appropriate amount of detail. Not everyone is ready or needs to know all the details.

You must also be honest about how much you are willing to hear. If you can separate the past from the present, and you believe people do change for the better, then someone's history may not be an issue for you.

Tell me about your past relationships?

_____

_____

_____

Circle your compatibility score   1   3   5

Question 46

Commitment

What weather will you weather?

Are you a fair weather lover who is only interested in the good times? Will you remain committed in stormier climates if your partner loses their job, their health declines or they face a major change in their life? Do you want an all-seasons mate or a casual friend for the good times or just a sex buddy?

It might be too early to know how either of you will react to a crisis in your relationship, but knowing your willingness and ability to hang in during tough times in the past is a sign of the commitment you can make to another person.

I asked Stephanie, a thirty-something-year-old lady, how she would know when she was in love. She replied, "If I have been dating someone for a few weeks or months and they said they were falling in love with me, I know it is not true. Unless we have faced some adversity together, the rest is an infatuation."

Is your goal in finding a mate to have someone rescue you from your life? If so, that may lead to trouble. Ideally, we should each be capable of looking after ourselves. However, our partner can certainly offer comfort, encouragement and a shoulder to lean on if the weather changes.

Joanna is youthful in appearance and attitude and fun to be with. She has discovered that it is easy to attract men but most do not stay very long. Joanna suffers from severe migraines that sometimes leave her bedridden for a week at a time. It has not been easy to keep full time employment. However, she admits that once men realize she needs them to care for her when a migraine strikes, most do not stay very long. Joanna needs a caretaker and finding an all seasons partner is her goal.

Diane fell in love with David, and they talked about marriage and started house hunting.

She made it clear that they should find a place that was not only within their budget, but also sustainable if one of them left for any reason. She was making a plan in case their seasons changed down the road. David found this refreshing and agreed they should live within their means and not be house rich and living poor.

Do you know your lover's state of health? Are they honest enough to share the state of their health early in the relationship? Can you accept someone who has a serious illness or condition? This could affect how you live together, your expenses and your future plans for travel, career, family and residence.

Janet has Crohn's disease, a digestive disorder. She met Tim and they fell in love. He realized early she could not maintain a full time job. He had a good career and was willing to support them both. They have been married for five years and are happy and compatible.

Are you committed enough to your partner and your own relationship to hang in regardless of what weather you endure?

You may want to explore your lover's position on commitment and how they would deal with sudden changes to get a flavor of what the future may hold. You can discuss the following scenarios:

1. A job transfer to another city.
2. A sick relative who needs to move in for a month or two.

3. A workmate's unsolicited advances.
4. An injury that prevents you from working for six weeks.
5. A partner who travels out of town three out of four weeks each month.

Your level of commitment is essential to the foundation of your relationship. The more you know, share and reflect about your goals and your willingness to adjust if the weather changes, the better your chances of navigating through stormy times.

What weather will you weather?

_____

_____

_____

What weather will your partner weather?

_____

_____

_____

Circle your compatibility score   1   3   5

Question 47

Commitment

What are your deal breakers?

Do you have a list of deal breakers? Where do you draw the line that would make you pause, or seriously re-think remaining in this relationship?

Infidelity, lying, stealing, dishonesty, criticism, and extreme control can all be deal breakers.

Would you also include violence, physical or mental abuse on your list?

Some of us have a tendency to rationalize, give the benefit to the other person, or convince ourselves that their bad behavior is a one-time aberration. You need to know what standard of care you desire and stick to it. Yes, everyone makes mistakes, but when it comes to mistreatment, you need to know your boundaries.

When Robert dated Martina, she shared that she had been married twice and had two children with two different men. Robert was fine with that and liked both her daughters. Then one weekend, Martina seemed preoccupied and stressed. Robert asked what was wrong. After some hesitation, she revealed she had a big court case on

Monday that could result in her getting some money from a former business partner. She was nervous about going to court to try and settle this debt. Robert offered to go with her for support, but she declined his offer. Later, she revealed the man she was facing in court was actually her third husband. Robert was hurt by her dishonesty and stepped back. In the weeks that followed, he uncovered a series of lies that added to his deal breaker list. He chose to move on and find someone who wanted an open and honest relationship.

Mac fell in love with Eve, or at least he thought he did. He would drink occasionally at a social function, but rarely anywhere else. Eve liked getting high and often got stoned when they were together. After three months Mac realized this was a deal breaker. It took him two more months of effort trying to help her face her addiction, but she chose the drugs over him and he moved on.

Are there any issues that fall into your deal breaker basket? Some hurdles between you may need some discussion and can be resolved, but if they are true deal breakers, are you prepared to hit the road and not look back?

What are your deal breakers? Make your list....

_____

_____

_____

Circle your compatibility score   1   3   5

Question 48

Commitment

Can you see yourself with this person in five years?

I was having some serious issues with communication and finances with a lady I lived with. We sought out a kind and insightful counseling couple who helped us to discover and explore the issues that were creating the tension in our lives.

At one point, they asked me if I could see myself in this tense, combative and energy-depleting relationship in five years. My immediate response was, "No, not even for five more minutes." That question revealed how bad the dynamic was between us. Unfortunately, I did not have the courage to end the relationship that day and continued hoping things would change. It took another two years for me to accept there was no happiness on the horizon and our relationship had become toxic.

At the beginning of a new relationship, once the cloud of elation has cleared a little, your hormones have calmed down, and the real issues between you begin to surface, take a good look at your future together. Are the pillars of this relationship strong enough to sustain you for the next five years and hopefully the rest of your lives?

If you are not looking for marriage, or a long-term commitment, then this question may be irrelevant at this stage of the relationship.

However, if you are feeling really good about this person and the pillars of Chemistry, Cash, Caring, Communication, and Commitment are lined up, this question needs serious reflection.

Imagine what your life will be like in five years. Will you be in the same home, city, and career? Will there be children in your future? Can you see yourself creating a life filled with similar goals, stronger feelings and greater love for each other? Can you envision the habits, faults and concerns you have about each other being accepted, resolved or still challenging? What are your expectations of yourself and your life with this person you may marry?

Jenny was a school teacher and lived close to her parents and had a tight knit group of long time friends. She met Bruce, a musician who travelled quite a bit. She told me she was attracted to his outgoing personality, creative abilities and out-of-the-box lifestyle. They saw each other during the week and only on weekends when he was in town performing. Although they had strong feelings for each other and made some adjustment to their schedules to be together, she realized he was just beginning to peak in his career and had goals of a much bigger life chasing his musical dreams. She really wanted a stable life, home and children. She realized a five-year plan together was not workable and they parted.

Earlier, I asked the question, "Why do you want to be married?" Too often, couples get lost in the planning of the big wedding day festivities and forget about their life together. Taking some time to discuss your life after that day will be invaluable and coupled with this question may provide some insight to your future you may not have explored.

These are not easy questions to answer early in a relationship, but if you have some idea of what you want your future to be, and how this person fits into that life, you can at least consider the answers.

Can you see yourself with this person in five years?

_____

_____

_____

Circle your compatibility score   1   3   5

QUESTION 49

Commitment

What are the qualities of the marriages you admire?

What couples do you know who have good and long-term marriages?

Admiring those who have successfully created healthy, loving and committed relationships may inspire or reveal to you the qualities that you aspire to have in yours.

Coming from a broken home and growing up with a divorced, single parent or a parent with multiple partners will influence choices and strategies in your relationships. Growing up in a stable, caring home, where both parents exhibited respect, kindness and love for each other, also shapes your choices and willingness to commit to another person.

Modeling others can be helpful, provided what you are admiring resonates with you and you are willing to invest the time, energy and commitment to create that kind of union.

Glen's parents have been married for over fifty years. They still live independently and enjoy their lives together. He has a brother and sister who are happily married too, and Glen admits, "It's been a challenge to find a partner for the long-term." He has been divorced twice and is not anxious to get back into the dating scene.

Tony also has parents that have been married for almost fifty years that exemplify the picture of love and caring for each other. He confesses, he had a different goal than his folks and was more interested in meeting women he could learn and grow from and did not think it was possible in one person or relationship. He shares that he was married early and had two children who he loves dearly, but admits, "I was in a deep trance in my early twenties and had no idea of who I was or what I wanted. I met a nice girl, we thought marriage was what we were suppose to do, so we blindly jumped it."

Having a history in your life of loving and stable parents in a long-term marriage does not guarantee success for you, but identifying the qualities you admire in successful relationships may give you some insight and tools to strive for.

We also run the risk of replicating those we witnessed, who were dysfunctional, incompatible or downright nasty towards each other. This can leave us with a perception that marriage does not work.

Thomas told me he was once married, and after a very ugly divorce has chosen to stay clear of committing to any one woman. He states, "I am trouble for anyone who wants a long term monogamous guy." This clarity helps him find what he wants and he seems happy having relationships that remain casual and fun and he avoids any talk of a future with his lady friends. This works for him.

Gene and Barbara are retired educators who enjoy golfing and hiking together. They have three children and six grandchildren, and are very involved in their family's lives. They make an effort to help with each generation of their clan whenever they can. I asked them what the secret of their forty-eight year marriage was and they said, "We realized early that we wanted to be each other's best friend." They also shared that they discussed how they would handle money in their marriage and thankfully were on the same page.

Jay's parents divorced when he was quite young. His mother, who never remarried, raised him. She did not date very often either. She dedicated her life to his well-being. He saw his father frequently and maintained a good relationship with him. His Dad remarried and Jay established a healthy and loving relationship with his step-Mom. He admits, because of what he witnessed as a child, it was sometimes difficult to know where his allegiance should be, but eventually realized he had the love of two mothers. He decided that he would try and practice the traits he admired in all his parents in any relationship he began.

Previous generations had a stronger sense of commitment to each other and the institution of marriage. Walking away at the first sign of trouble was rarely considered. Today, we live in a more disposable society and some couples are ready to bail at the first sign of difficulty.

We have more options today to explore relationships before making a commitment. But, once we choose to make that commitment, it will serve us well to look at those we admire and use some of their strategies to work through the challenges we encounter.

I know of one couple in their eighties, who have known each other since high school, and continue to share a marriage full of life and love. Whenever I am with them, I feel happy, inspired and marvel at the aura of care between them.

What have these lifelong couples learned about dealing with challenge and change, as they hold hands for decades together? Interviewing or studying couples you admire will reveal some insights that may come in handy as you look for a love match.

Committing to the marriage first beyond everything else reduces your chance to abandon ship when the weather changes. Knowing what you want above all else and what you are willing to truly commit to makes it easier to save a marriage, because the many distractions that come our way can be easily placed lower on the priority list behind the importance of the marriage.

What are the qualities of the marriages you admire?

_____

_____

_____

Circle your compatibility score   1   3   5

Caring compatibility Rating Review

You have now completed all the questions on the Compatibility pillar — Commitment.

Total the number of #1s = little in common, #2s = some things in common and #3s = very compatible and insert below.

1 ____ 3 ____ 5 ____

You have now reviewed 49 questions. Congratulations.

It is now your turn to ask a question of yourself or your lover that may not be included in the five pillars of compatibility of Love Match. Please write your 50th question and why this is an important one for you. I would appreciate you emailing me your question so others can benefit from your insight. Lovematch50@gmail.com Thank you.

QUESTION 50

Create your own question here.

You have reviewed the fifty questions of Love Match and may be wondering if this book was too technical an exercise. You may ask, "What happened to romance, serendipity, the spontaneity of two souls meeting across a crowded room? Where is the fun and adventure of a chance encounter?"

I believe all those wonderful encounters are possible and exciting and I encourage you to embrace them. I have simply offered a toolbox of questions to review while you are falling into trance with this new person.

Your chances of finding and sustaining a passionate and compatible relationship have just improved by having this checklist to consult.

Staying conscious and knowing what works for you in your life will help keep that flame alive, the passion real, and the realities of sharing this grand adventure with another soul manageable, as you open your heart and mind to the greatest relationship of your life.

I wish you a wonderful Love Match.

To share stories or contact the author: www.stevebrass.com or lovematch50@gmail.com

19622261R00123

Made in the USA
Charleston, SC
03 June 2013